Crossing the Desert

Lent and Conversion

James Keating

D1366357

Liguori
ONE LIGUORI DRIVE
LIGUORI MO 63057-9999

Dedication

To Sister Colleen Walsh, C.S.A.,
and
Rev. Thomas Holahan, C.S.P.

In gratitude for their faithful witness to
Christ and service to his Church.

Imprimi Potest:
Richard Thibodeau, C.Ss.R.
Provincial, Denver Province
The Redemptorists

ISBN 0-7648-0682-3
Library of Congress Catalog Card Number: 00-102603

Scripture quotations are from the *New Revised Standard Version of the Bible*, copyright © 1989 by the Division of Christian Education of the National Council of Churches of Christ in the USA. Used with permission. All rights reserved.

Excerpts from the English translation of *Rite of Penance* © 1974, International Committee on English in the Liturgy, Inc. All rights reserved.

To order, call 1-800-325-9521
www.liguori.org
www.catholicbooksonline.com

Cover design by Grady Gunter

Table of Contents

The Author

James Keating, Ph.D. is Associate Professor of Moral Theology in the School of Theology at the Pontifical College Josephinum in Columbus, Ohio. He is the author of *Pure Heart, Clear Conscience: Living the Catholic Moral Life* (Our Sunday Visitor, 1999) and *Moral Formation in the Parish* (Alba House, 1998).

Acknowledgments

I would like to thank Elizabeth Kampmeier, M.Div., Research Assistant at the Pontifical College Josephinum, for her careful preparation of this text and for her continued support and encouragement of all my professional writing.

I would also like to thank those who read early drafts of this book and whose helpful comments have made this a better work: Rev. Anthony Ciorra, William Hinger, Constance Michalec, Beverly Lane, and Rev. Kevin Louis.

CHAPTER ONE

The Desert of Consumerism

L ent is not what it used to be." An elderly gentleman said this to me as we both waited to have our hair cut at a local barber. We had been talking about incidentals and then got around to asking what the other did for a living. He was a retired accountant. When I told him I teach theology in a seminary, he asked all kinds of questions about the faith we mutually shared. Since we had just entered Holy Week, he began speaking about Lent. "Sometimes I feel that there is nothing in between Ash Wednesday and Easter today except life as usual. I don't remember it that way forty years ago. No, I remember it felt like we all went through something together. Lent is not what it used to be."

I was struck by this statement and how I, too, agreed with him, not that I have any memories of a rigorous lenten penance from my past, but that it seems as if life in Lent is "life as usual" and that we do not go through it together as a community.

What he said about Lent stayed with me all day. What is the purpose of Lent? Is it simply a season of "life as usual" except for Ash Wednesday and Holy Week? Is there any way to have its holy meaning penetrate the rival cultural interests put forward by economic, leisure, and consumer needs? I wondered whether Lent had become yet another secular season in our culture—like "Back to School" time, or the continuous market plea to "Buy Now!...Stock up now!"—with Lent holding even less impact because it doesn't ask us to spend any money. Lent is a season that can come and pass without having any economic impact whatsoever, with one exception: I notice more advertisements for fish.

Even the marketing of fish, however, is a kind of a remnant of former Lents, holding little or no power to turn our minds to penance. One can see the impotence of the fish symbol by driving past a Red Lobster™ restaurant on a Friday in Lent and seeing it packed with people "doing penance" by avoiding a beef dinner. The fish symbol has lost its punch, its relevance to the self-denial of Lent. Can we revisit the meaning of Lent and try to find its purpose for today? Lent is not simply a season of avoidance; it is a season of new life, a springtime of the soul. In the pages that follow, let us see why.

Meditation Room:
Recall your most promising Lent. Why did it or did it not reach fulfillment?

There may be many different approaches to a renewed understanding of what Lent means in a life of faith. One could study it through the liturgies of Lent. It could be approached through the study of Scripture. I, however, will highlight the meaning of Lent through the call for moral conversion, which of course includes the liturgical and scriptural approaches as well. Scripture and the liturgy both call for repentance from sin.

The word "lent" originated in Middle English and means "springtime." In the turning from sin and the consequent embracing of moral goodness, one knows a moral "springtime." We are invited to a moral rebirth. Moral conversion, more than the changing of seasons, underscores the spring of *spiritual* living. Just like in the seasonal spring, in the spiritual spring one has to pass through a spiritual autumn chill of internal struggle and a winter's death of the ego so as to come to live the new life of virtue that awaits us in the promises of Easter. These promises hold out the hope that in leaving the old life of sin behind, nothing is lost; rather, we awaken to truth and the real meaning of life. If we can trust God enough to see us through the winter to the springtime of moral conversion, the immoral life will be revealed for what it truly is: an empty and superficial existence supported only by a veneer of selfish satisfaction.

Pope John Paul II has highlighted a key theme of Lent as it relates to moral conversion: "There is an urgent need to work for the good of others and to be ready to *lose oneself*—in the Gospel sense—in order to *serve others*" ("Identification with the Poor" [1991 lenten message] in *Origins* 20:32 (17 January 1991) 524 [author's emphasis]).

To lose oneself is a vital lenten theme in the sense that one is called to discipline the selfish part of the self and develop selflessness. It is the selfish part of the self that needs to fast and do penance by visiting the "desert" of Lent and thus foster a growing dependence upon God. The result of such a dying to selfishness is a blossoming of service to others in need.

Lent ends at the Holy Thursday table with our commemoration of Jesus serving others by washing the disciples' feet. Throughout Lent we *do* things or *refrain from* doing things in order to become detached from the selfish self and attached to God and others by slowly appropriating a servant disposition. As the disciples were scandalized by Jesus' servant disposition toward them, we too continue to resist the meaning of discipleship that calls us to serve others through virtuous action. We resist this call to act out of the moral and theological virtues because it carries with it an unrelenting call to move beyond selfishness. We are summoned to think of others' needs in the same serious way we attend to our own.

This call to attend to others in their needs contains the drama of moral living. Will we give up our agenda when love and moral goodness require it? Or will we cling to the selfish self out of fear that our own demands will be unmet? The act of handing the self over to God truly establishes a firm base for reducing selfish fear, thus preparing us for doing good to and with others. It is this fear that truly represents the sin in us.

This sin is so deep within us that simply willing it out of our hearts is impossible. Ultimately, we need to yield our entire self over to Christ, who saves us even from this deep enslavement to fear. Our faith teaches us that it is safe to stop thinking of the self and think instead of others, because God is thinking of all of us in love and mercy. In this way, religious faith grounds the moral life; it gives us the courage and the reason needed to reach beyond the self and serve others by being virtuous in their presence.

The need to trust God is so paramount to moral and spiritual growth that a powerful religious symbol developed and became enshrined in Scripture to characterize this trust. This symbol is the desert. The desert immediately brings to mind aridity and aloneness—a vast, dry, isolated existence. It is this symbol, however, that carries the strongest of all claims: If you dare to come into the desert and open your heart to God—invite God to *be* God in God's full providence—you will know salvation. The desert becomes the stage for God to woo us, to call the Church into union with God's own self.

The Church gives us the seasonal time of Lent as a desert experience so we will come to depend on God. Come into Lent and know the salvation of God, just as Moses and the Hebrews knew God's care in the desert and Jesus knew the Father's protection from vice in the desert of temptation.

Meditation Room:

What is your most vivid experience of entering the desert,
of entering a period of time in a relationship
that called for deep trust?
What does "being in a desert time" mean to you?

God's providence does not depend upon our ability to provide for ourselves and/or control the activities of others or ourselves. It only demands that we be *available* to God *working in us*. This cooperative availability will bring about the needed moral and spiritual changes our growth in holiness requires. As we resist going into desert wastelands, we resist going into the liturgical, devotional, and service aspects of Lent. We ask: "What will this time demand of me?…What will I lose out on?…What will I miss in my usual daily patterns of life if I go into the desert?…What will I accomplish?"

There is a fear that motivates these questions. If we look at the area of work and business, for example, we see that vacation time is getting shorter and shorter for many professionals. Many forego Sunday or Sabbath "down time." We cannot rest because we are afraid someone will get the upper hand on new data or develop a new approach on a project. The reality of "I can be replaced" looms large in our consciousness. In an economic culture, religious realities like Lent appear quaint, dated, and not really "useful."

Of course, no one is asking us to go into a literal desert, like Moses and Jesus did. Rather, we are asked to look for the desert that has come to us in our daily life. We are called to look for those times when we must rely on divine providence to give us the strength necessary to do *one more* load of laundry, to get up *one more* day and go to a job that provides little more than a paycheck, or to listen to *one more* child's bedtime story. In these sometimes dry and ordinary events, we are invited to trust that God is there, working to bring us closer to divinity and farther away from the death grip of selfishness. Lent asks whether we trust in God alone. Can we abandon the illusion of human self-sufficiency and live in obedience to God alone? (See Andrew Louth, *The Wilderness of God*, Nashville: Abingdon [1997] 39.)

For those in the Church who live in the Western world and command middle income salaries or higher, the question of self-sufficiency and the spiritual dangers it brings are not pious cautions but a matter of life or death for the soul. We know all too well our ordered lives of family, schedule, work, and rest. Even though many complain of the "rat race" of urban and suburban living, behind the frantic activity is much routine and even boredom. In some strange way, we must admit that we like the boredom. We affirm the routine and the familiar: the same shopping venues, restaurants, sporting activities, and consuming and buying patterns. We feel a strange comfort in the fact that there is a GAP™ store in every city and franchised restaurants repeated endlessly across the country. We affirm the fact that we want the same clothes, the same cars, and the same housing as everyone else.

We also can sense a restlessness, however, a small struggle or revolt, as more and more people look to break out of the routine to find the "more," the "different," and the "unusual." This rebellion against "more of the same" makes itself known in persons looking for new religions, "spirituality" detached from churches, angels in our dreams and in our statues, pictures, and knickknacks—but not necessarily seen as carrying divine messages and commands. We are bored. We want the feeling of ecstasy but not the price or the way of ecstasy, namely, the desert, Lent, the cross of commitment. In our search for a relevant spirituality of "seeking," we fear the very thing to be found on this search that is demanded by God and by the truth: the death of the "fat relentless ego" (Iris Murdoch, *The Sovereignty of Good*, NY: Schocken Books [1970] 52).

Meditation Room:

Recall an event you engaged in or a commitment you made
that caused some physical or mental suffering.
Was the suffering worth the reward?
What made the suffering worth it?

The search for a life beyond self-sufficiency that is beginning to stir in popular Western culture must be affirmed, and the Church can direct this search more explicitly. The American consumerist culture has reached a saturation point. We can see this in the empty strip malls and closed shops that dot the country, promises of meaning and pleasure worn out by our own overuse and their inability to satisfy.

The emptiness of these shopping deserts does not, in itself, herald the end of the materialism that masquerades as moral and spiritual truth. One can find just as quickly the new mall in the land of suburban sprawl, or another new one rising out of what was once farmland. This former farmland now provides not simply consumer goods but also the false hope found in the obligatory *spiritual* promises of the market, the false promises of "new and improved," or youth, beauty, friendship, and the "more," if we will simply buy certain products and frequent certain stores. Unlike Abraham and Moses who traveled into the unknown solely on faith, we continue to develop artificial environments of control, repetition, and self-sufficiency. Why listen for and to God's voice in the desert, we think, when we already have the promised manna in our products? These products assure fulfillment; however, they do not deliver.

God gives the lenten desert for our own good. We enter this space so that from our isolation we may come to call out to God. God encounters us as a people no longer glowing in self-sufficiency but humbled by the reality known only in dependency upon God's providential hand. Lent is a time to get our priorities straight: to seek first the kingdom of God, and then all else will be given to us (Matthew 6:33). In other words, God calls us away from the marketing, fashion, and economic illusions built around our legitimate and not so legitimate needs in order to remind us that true happiness is found only in right relation to God.

We are so busy avoiding ultimate questions in our frantic lives of motion that we leave no room for God to get a word in edgewise. Just as the over-committed business woman or man resists the thought of time away from work and the meaning it gives, so the believer finds excuses and rationalizations for not being engaged by God in the lenten space offered by prayer, fasting, devotion, and good works. These disciplines offer a space, a desert within, through which God can reach us again.

The Church gives us Lent so that we may allow God to find us again. God searches for us, much as God searched for Adam and Eve in the garden. The desert represents a time of renewal. It is a liturgical and personal second honeymoon with God. We clear the way for true encounter like a married couple who retreats to a hotel for a long-needed rest in each other's arms. "Where have you been?" they ask one another. Once again they ask the same questions they asked upon first meeting: "Who are you, and why do you affect me so?"

Before the second honeymooners repeated these basic questions of intimacy, however, they had to go through a resistance to the call to self-offering. "I can't get away, honey; not now, the calendar is so full. Let's plan something later."… "I would love to go, but so many people are depending upon me." The lover calls, however, and woos the beloved out into the desert, where first there is grumbling and regret: "Why did I come? There is nothing here but emptiness, a 'space' I have known for years, YOU."

In Lent, God encourages the beloved to look again, to feel again, to trust again. "You will lose nothing by seeking me and being with me. All of your heart's desires will be satisfied; just abide with me now in trust." What appears at first as barren to the desert entrant, soon discloses itself to be filled with blooms of new life. Hence the paradox of the spring-desert image of Lent. Here is the power of God in its utmost: Where one thought there was *no life*, God *brings life*.

The desert, the end of self-sufficiency, is not death of the self but the beginning of communion between the self and the beloved, and between the self and God. Out of this loving communion comes new life. Even in and among the cultural and spiritual deserts of American consumerism, even here, where promises lie unfulfilled and boredom reigns, God can bring life. God can sustain the man and woman of faith to trust totally in God's self, and can see them peacefully through the next empty consumer trend. Similarly, just when a couple thinks there is no life left in their barren space of a marriage, waiting in that space with God can bring new life, a new perspective on love's demands and rewards.

Meditation Room:

What most prevents you from believing that God can bring good out of evil, life out of death?

Jesus tells us not to worry about tomorrow, for what is needed will be provided (Matthew 6:11, 34). If we truly live in Lent, we can yield over our concerns and come to trust that God will provide. The frightening question is: *What* will God provide? Certainly, God will not provide what the marketing companies tell us we so desperately need in their ads in Sunday's newspaper. No, the desert will provide only the space God needs to offer us salvation. Those saints who live always in Lent, always disposed to trust the Spirit in the formation of their character by the Spirit, seek nothing other than God. God's economy does not announce what God has *in store* for us but, like a good lover, surprises us. "What no eye has seen, nor ear heard, nor the human heart conceived, what God has prepared for those who love him" (1 Corinthians 2:9).

What does God have *in store*, in stock, so to speak, for the Western consumer? This is a God who asks those dwelling in the desert of Lent not to store anything in their barns, because "this very night your life is being demanded of you"(Luke 12:20). Why do we cling to the self when the self is all we have to give away to God? Beyond any legitimate need for consumption and play, we begin to think we can commune with things and create environments in which we lose ourselves in gadgets, distractions, and toys. This only leaves us lonely. God is the enemy of loneliness and continually tries to get us to see that, even to the point of coming to share our loneliness in Jesus Christ. Our loneliness and alienation can be the desert from within which God calls to us.

In the desert, the ultimate symbol of loneliness, as we go searching for the one who will satisfy our hearts, we can find no substitute for God. The senses are denied the diversions of ordinary life, and we are forced to cry out. In this cry is our salvation. We do not cry out at the mall because we are immersed in things that tickle our fancy, divert our attention, and numb our restlessness to the point where meaningful questions no longer arise. In the desert, however, we feel our aloneness and our helplessness. In the desert, we face our limitations in a vast silence. Silence frightens us, and yet we see that it is in silence that God speaks most clearly (1 Kings 19:11-13).

Even the plentitude of the shopping mall can become the desert when, in our distress at the emptiness of things, we despair at finding meaning there. In that despair, that "loneliness in a crowd," we enter the desert and cry out. Hearing our cry, God comes to us. Ultimately, we have learned from Christ that when our cry of the heart ascends to God, God listens. This is seen most clearly in Christ's cry from the cross, the ultimate desert, the ultimate Lent: "My God, my God, why have you forsaken me?" (Matthew 27:46). We, too, can cry out from the emptiness of much of the popular culture and see that God does not abandon us but, through grace, empowers us to rise again, to be the salt and light within it (Matthew 5:13-14).

Meditation Room:

**Recall your most powerful experience
of having been listened to by God.**

Thus, Lent is a time of entering into our real identity before God. Oftentimes, this place of knowing our real identity, our faults and our virtues, can feel like we have entered a desert, a wasteland. We can become so alienated from our real self that we fear knowing where we truly stand in the life of faith, hope, and love. We resist being encountered by God in the desert. There is, however, nothing to fear. Lent is a time given to us by the Church within the liturgical year to invite us into a deeper dependency upon God. It presents an opportunity for us to disengage from any attachments we have fostered over the year that are beneath our dignity and thus threaten our communion with God and others.

Since Lent demands the one thing we do not want to part with—the self—we rationalize it as a "waste": a waste of time when I could be working, a waste of energy when I could be playing, a waste of opportunity when I could be buying. Working, playing, and buying have their rightful and useful places, but they also can expand disproportionately out of their proper places and become all consuming. In the Western world, we have become a new "species," as some have recently said: "*Homo economicus*." The market defines us.

Lent wants to remind us of our *real* identity. At first appearance a seeming "obligation," Lent is actually a great gift. Are we brave enough to enter this desert, and then let it affect us so deeply as to turn us away from sin and false identities, turn us toward communion with the living God? The Church presents this season to us every year because it is hoped that *this* year will be our year to say "Yes" to Lent's call to repentance.

Lent should not be something we go through alone, but *together*. As the Hebrews wandered the desert for forty years, so we should enter Lent through the ecclesial community and share its challenges with brothers and sisters in Christ. Lent should not be what the elderly man in the barbershop characterized as "life as usual." With our goal being moral conversion, let us now turn to see how God can facilitate that conversion when we take on a "lenten mind."

CHAPTER TWO

The Desert
of Ordinary Life

People do not separate their union with Christ from their ordinary life, but actually grow closer to him by doing their work
according to God's will....The layperson, at one and the same
time a believer and a citizen of the world, has only a single conscience, a christian conscience, by which to be guided continually in both domains [Church and secular society]" ("Decree on
the Apostolate of Lay People" in *Vatican Council II: The Basic
Sixteen Documents*, ed. Austin Flannery, OP, Northport, NY:
Costello [rev. 1996] 4,5).

People have a tendency to try to make life easier by separat-
ing "real life" from "religion." No doubt it is difficult trying to
be Christian twenty-four hours a day, especially when some persons in the daily company we keep are not interested in trying, or
are benignly oblivious to the call to be publicly Catholic. After
all, religion is for Sunday, isn't it?

Yes, of course, religion involves Sunday worship. The worship we participate in on Sunday, however, if not deeply connected to what we do Monday through Saturday, becomes
simply a meaningless obligation. Worship then becomes an

obligation for which we can give no good reason to fulfill. One of the first steps in any moral conversion rooted in religious faith is to find ways to get reconnected to the Sunday liturgy, and to keep the Mass connected to the other six days. It may appear to be a big job to do so, but in reality it is not. It appears difficult for some of us because our thinking has been focused on relegating religion only to holy places or church (building) people.

In order to deepen the religious meaning of our daily life, we are invited by the Church to find ways to see and cherish the holy in the ordinary, and then to celebrate that presence at the very source of sacramental holiness itself, the eucharistic liturgy. The transforming quality of worship is that the more we participate in it, and having seen God in the ordinary, the more meaning it takes on and the less it appears as a drudgery or pointless obligation. The reverse is also true: The more we endeavor to listen to God at worship, the more our heart is attuned to the divine presence at home, at work, at social gatherings. We then begin to see God everywhere, as do all those who are called to holiness.

This awareness of God in the everyday is not an oppressive presence, looming over us with codes and laws, but a loving presence calling us to a deeper fidelity to human dignity, a fidelity that ultimately results in our happiness. The more we are vulnerable to God's presence, the more we want to be good and happy in God's sight. This really is the great secret of the saints: their *desire* for moral goodness in the midst of their *relationship* with God as known in *ordinary* living and regular worship.

There is no trick to becoming good and holy; it is in fact the *destiny* of all who are of God. God wants us to be converted morally, and therefore is not stingy with divine grace and assistance. This grace-filled presence in the ordinariness of our days gives testimony to God's generous call, offering us communion with our Creator in and through moral goodness.

Even though the number of people attending church services in the United States has declined in recent years, we still retain one of the highest percentages of worshiping populations in the Western world. Nevertheless, on occasion one hears that people are disappointed with each week's "experience" of the liturgical celebration. It seems rote; children and adults alike feel bored. I had one altar server tell me that he likes to serve Mass because in doing so it "feels like it's over faster." This is hardly a testimony to his finding God in worship!

It is true for most of us, however, that on occasion the Eucharist seems like something we attend only so we can "get it over with." Sundays appear to hold out the promise of more interesting things to do than praising God. Therefore, we have ambiguous feelings about worship; we show up but are not quite sure why—after all, it is not always entertaining, and often we say we "don't get anything out of it."

Meditation Room:

Does public and official Church liturgy hold the key to your intimacy with Christ? Why or why not?

The Mass, however, is not about entertainment; it is about adoration and facilitating communion with the Father through Christ. The goal of worship is not to be interesting or entertaining, but to give us the opportunity to praise and adore God. Moreover, it is not in the nature of adoration to bring on boredom.

So what is the problem? Eucharist becomes irrelevant for many of us because we forget that if we do not seek communion with God throughout the week, we will be going to the house of a stranger on Sunday. Worship is only relevant to our lives, and therefore interesting to us, if we participate by seeking deeper intimacy with the God we have loved throughout the week. The eucharistic celebration can be seen as the culmination of small acts of love and communion that we have had with God all week.

When I was a small boy, my family would visit a distant aunt a couple of times each year. On the day that we were to go and visit her, my mother would call my brother, sisters, and me in from playing with our friends. No way did I want to go to my aunt's house; I had nothing in common with her. We hardly saw her, so even building common experiences was impossible, but off we went…reluctantly. I can remember sitting at her kitchen table, staring at the plate of food in front of me and pushing the peas around, while wishing I was back at home playing with my friends.

Is this not what the Mass is like for some of us? Certainly, it seems so for the altar server who wanted it to "go faster," and for the people who know only boredom at Mass. When we are with good friends, people with whom we share common interests, do we think, "I hope this ends soon so I can get to something better"? No, we luxuriate in their presence. We sincerely regret when our time is over, or if they have to excuse themselves earlier than we had hoped. We want them with us just so that we can *be* together.

Eucharist is the place where friends of Jesus beg him to stay just so that they can *be* together (see Jn 4:40). This communion with Christ has to be cultivated all week long, however, just like any friendship. If we do so, Christ's friendship will take us deep into intimacy with him and with his Father. He will show us how much he loves us, and how willing he is to give himself for us, even unto death.

Once we realize that it is not in the nature of worship to be entertaining, I can think of only one reason that we would be bored at Mass: we are visiting a stranger. It does not have to be that way, however. This divine friend is waiting for us every day in prayer, Scripture reading, and service to the poor and needy. If we cultivate this friendship all week, when Sunday comes around we will not be simply "pushing the peas around" on our plate at church and wishing we were elsewhere.

Thus, a first step to moral conversion is to connect the daily moral decisions we make to the reality of Jesus' rapt listening to his Father upon the cross, and to his ultimate Resurrection as represented in the eucharistic liturgy. This is the great gift that Jesus left us, and within it is the whole power of God's love for all people in the ordinary circumstances of their lives. By adoring the Father through the sacramental self-offering of Christ in the Eucharist, we can become involved in this mystery of God's love for us.

By participating in this sacrament, we are bid to not simply commune with Christ, but to "go in peace." We are charged to go into the everyday world and bring peace to the world. Since we receive Christ in holy Communion, we are to be Christ for our friends, coworkers, family members, and even strangers, and enemies. It will be Christ dwelling within us that supports us in this transformation of character, a transformation that ultimately affects the character of society as well. The Christian moral life is not mainly about *willing* goodness; it is about *receiving it, then enacting it with and out of the power of Christ* who dwells within the Church.

Meditation Room:

Has a moral virtue, such as courage, temperance,
or chastity, ever been given to you by God
with little or no effort on your part?
What gifts has God bestowed upon you?

Also helpful in fostering conversion from sin is knowledge of the consequences of our current pattern of behavior in daily life. Moral growth will be difficult if we have no cognizance of our present state of virtue. This does not need to be a very formal or rigorous discipline, encompassing journal keeping or spiritual direction or retreats or similar exercises, although these activities can be helpful and do aid our growth in holiness.

I have found, however, that when I recommend these activities to people, they embrace the idea eagerly and look forward to "the time when they can" immerse themselves in these disciplines; for most, that means sometime after retirement. The pace of active lay life simply leaves little time or opportunity to engage in anything more than going to church on Sunday, and perhaps some light Bible or other spiritual reading and a rare but fruitful attendance at an adult education course or lecture in the parish. Thus, we are left to mine the contents of our normal routine and see how God is teaching us daily about the consequences of our behaviors. As Vatican II reminds us, it will be through the very performance of our daily tasks that we will grow in holiness.

In order to look for the fruits of our current moral behavior, we first have to be open to receive the truth about ourselves. Bad news about our own character is very difficult to hear, much less embrace. If we are not supple and vulnerable to the truth, we will stay where we are morally, stagnating in the unhealthy pond of our present vices. We first have to desire to listen to the truth about ourselves.

Do we have that desire? If not, perhaps this daily prayer can help soften the heart that is closed to any painful information about our character. "O God, today I am living for you and for the good of others; please instruct me on how my own attitude and behavior makes it harder for goodness to be present in the world." This is a simple prayer, but it will carry power when prayed as a regular part of our life. It softens the hardened heart and opens the ear of the conscience to listen to the truth about ourselves. Over time, and in grace, we will become attuned to our own uneasiness about our behavior; we will take clues from others' words, body language, and level of presence in our lives. These truths can tell us whether we are aiming toward virtue or simply limiting our presence to egoistic concerns or self-hating obsessions.

I have a tendency to worry about money. This anxiety can reach quite a zenith on payday, when—after the bills are paid—there is little left to exist on for the month. Being married, it is easy to take my anxiety out on my wife. I used to either grow quiet or, conversely, angry, and she would bear the brunt of it. This obviously had a very negative effect upon our marriage. Rarely would I simply and honestly say to her: "I am a little anxious about money this month."

On those occasions when I did say something about my concern, she would point out how well we were doing and help me calm down for the moment. The important point here is that her words would help me "for the moment." The reality of the situation would intellectually be heard, but affectively I was still nervous. One day, however, I stumbled across a truth known to many but new to me. When anxiety would arise within me, I would simply say to Marianne, my wife, "You know, I love you," and she would smile, and I would know that everything really *was* all right.

Despite real suffering and lack of material goods in peoples' lives, acknowledging the presence of love within their lives can be a dynamic healing power. Attending to my actions that were born of exaggerated anxiety, I saw that their fruit was damaging to my family. It pleased me to be anxious, for some neurotic reason, but it really did nothing to bring my family into deeper communion with one another. I began to simply *say* what was more *fully true* about our family than our financial dearth: that I love my family. In actually speaking that reality at a time of heightened anxiety, I lessened my own nervousness and affirmed the larger-than-financial truth about my life: I am one with my wife and children.

This moral-emotional example from my own life highlights the fact that we need to attend to the consequences of our behavior and note their effects. On some occasions we can do this on our own, but in some cases others may bring the fruit of our behavior to our attention. Either way, we still need a softened heart to hear the truth.

I recall another example relevant to my point. I was shopping in a grocery store with a friend for some last minute items, just before we both went home to have a dinner that Marianne was preparing for us. My friend Thomas said: "I should bring something home to Marianne, wine and flowers." I showed him where our "usual" wine was located, and then I grabbed a cheap bouquet of flowers wrapped in cellophane on the way to the register. He returned with a different brand of wine, very expensive, and looked with dismay at my "interpretation" of flowers. He left me at the register, and returned with twelve beautiful, fresh roses from the flower department. "How did you ever get married, Jim?" he asked. My stinginess was exposed in a lighthearted way, but nonetheless exposed. I listened, and learned a truth about myself.

Meditation Room:

When did God last teach you a truth about yourself through another person's word or deed?

In the Catholic imagination, our vocation to married or single life becomes the touchstone for moral growth. Any behavior or vice that diminishes the dignity of our vocation, as baptized married or single Catholics, is to become the primary signal indicating a need for moral conversion. The call to holiness is only given within the ordinary structure of the baptized married or single life. That is our way to salvation, and anything that pulls at that fabric is indeed morally and spiritually dangerous.

This is why Lent can be a wonderful time to strengthen our identity within our individual calls to marriage or the single life. Most of us are called to one of these two states, and they regulate our identity before God, even more so than our profession or work. It is necessary to remind ourselves of this, because Western culture tends to see one's work or professional identity as exhausting the full expression of a person's social worth. By emphasizing our *relational commitments* as primary—not our achievements—the Catholic Church becomes immediately countercultural in its call to moral conversion.

Are we, in fact, going deep within our sacramental life to find our dignity and thus transform culture accordingly, or are we going more deeply within our achievement commitments and therefore only conforming to culture? To even ask this question makes some of us very nervous, since our sacramental imagination is only anemically present within our day-to-day lives. More commonly, our economic and social imagination plays a larger role in determining the direction of our decisions. In order to facilitate moral-religious conversion in our lives, we must come to identify how our sacramental participation and identity fills our daily lives and orients us toward what is good and holy.

How do we begin to develop a sacramental mind in the midst of ordinary living? Our moral characters are formed by what we spend the most time thinking about and paying attention to. We cannot spend all day at liturgy, or in prayer before the Blessed Sacrament, or in service to the economically poor. We do, however, serve the needs of family and friends daily, and we do need to conform our daily life to the essence of the sacramental life— the encounter we have with Christ through the Church.

The most vital truth to remember for moral conversion is that we take the vocational sacraments with us wherever we go. I am always married; I am always baptized; and, in a sense, I am always in communion with Christ through my participation in the Eucharist. Our encounter with Christ is as close as our last act of love toward our child or spouse. We are *living* the sacramental life through our last prayer or act of charity toward an "enemy." Through a rhythmic pattern of explicit worship and daily commitment to the meaning of sacramental living, Catholics grow more deeply aware of God's merciful and life-changing presence in all things ordinary.

Lent becomes a time to cultivate our feeble sacramental imagination, as the opportunities for worship, prayer, meditation, service, and reconciliation increase over these forty days.

In a real way, Lent beckons us to go into the sacramental and the ordinary folds of our lives in ways that enrich both; we begin to live out of them simultaneously and more deeply. Truly, as Saint Paul exclaimed, we carry the "marks of Christ" (Galatians 6:17) within us every single day of our lives. This is true as a result of being given over to God in baptism, of being more richly conformed to Christ's self-offering on the cross through reconciliation and Eucharist, and in our particular vocations of commitment. To receive again our call from Christ during Lent, and to let that call resonate throughout the daily affairs of secular life, is the true gift of Lent to us.

Lent promises to introduce us once again to God and God's great love for us in Christ. In and through that love, we come to know ourselves again and feel restored. When we have emerged from the desert of Lent, we can then bring this restored self in Christ back to the ordinariness of our days, pouring some of his living water on those who feel they are stumbling through an arid time. Then, the ordinariness of family, work, and social commitments does not remain in the category of "more of the same." Rather, these ordinary moments take on a transcendent quality that reaches from a simple talk with a spouse on the back porch or a game of catch with the kids, to the grounding of those events in the ever-present and saving love of Christ. From such a consciousness, we will begin to truly thirst for moral goodness. No longer will moral living appear as simply an "ought." Moral conversion and living will become the desire of our hearts.

Meditation Room:

What "marks" do you carry with you daily
as a result of some difficulty in being faithful to Christ?

The lay vocation is a most dignified call from Christ. Publicly, its heart and soul is the summons from Christ to transform culture into a civilization of love, goodness, and truth. In many ways, the laity abide in places that clergy never engage in the normal course of their ministry.

Lent stands as that opportunity to go with Christ into the desert and dispel again the temptations to do or be anything but what the Father has called us to be, to listen only to every word that comes forth from the mouth of God (Matthew 4:1-11). In this fidelity, we witness to the change that can happen when individuals and cultures listen for the moral truth, engage it, and then choose to embody it.

Sometimes, a moral conversion may be prompted by looking at the lives of others around us or by attending to the lives of those who have died before us. Positively, we can see virtue in others and hope to emulate those virtues in our own unique way. Negatively, we can also see that sometimes peoples' lives just do not "hit the mark," and we can learn from the tragedy of their lives.

There was a long-time administrator, at a school I was tangentially associated with, who died after an illness. The day before her funeral, I was in the company of some of the secretarial staff of this college, and I asked them their feelings about this woman's death. I was surprised to hear that they had little sympathy for her. Apparently, she had treated them with great disrespect while they were in her employ. One administrative assistant even went so far as to say that he would not attend the funeral, because at funerals they always portray the person in a perfect light and he would "not be able to bear such a charade in the midst of a worship service."

This brief conversation with those employees had a lasting

effect upon me. Never before had I heard such blunt conversation regarding the character of a recently deceased person. None of the staff even made an attempt to put the late administrator in any kind of positive light. They were simply relieved that she was gone. Needless to say, this encounter with those college employees made me think about my own moral character. Who would want such things said of them after death? It was a chilling exchange.

Obviously, God has the full picture of that woman's life before the divine mercy and love, and in no way do human judgments on personal character ever totally encapsulate reality, but in all likelihood the judgments of those coworkers do represent some grain of truth representative of the deceased's character.

The only location for God to interact with us is deep within the ordinariness of our days. We are called to cherish the ordinary day, not because of its routine or common features, but because within this daily forum God reaches us through others, through worship, charity, and our relational commitments. Our daily lives carry an invitation from God to become morally good and holy; it is the only medium through which this invitation can come. Cherish the days.

CHAPTER THREE

Waiting in the Desert

Recently, a priest friend of mine blurted out that he was a workaholic and that—"for the sake of my soul"—he had better stop trying to control every little thing that goes on in his parish. He told me that his spiritual director counseled him to "leave space" for God to act, invite, instruct, and even do miracles. He was told: "You are so busy making sure that everything will turn out right that you leave no room for God's will; it's all your will." Obviously, this counsel was not given to promote sloth, but it was a plea from the Spirit to leave a space for prayer, for waiting, listening, and receiving.

Our heads are so filled with To Do lists that very little of what God may be wanting to do or teach us can get a hearing. This concept of "leaving space" for God is crucial in any call to moral conversion. One impetus for cooperating with a call to moral conversion is the realization that what has filled our minds might be selfish, less than noble, or simply wrong. What we know to be true most often motivates us to act, and we usually only know what is true by what we have filled our heads with. The goal of Christian moral conversion is to turn us away from inadequate or immoral sources of conscience formation and introduce us to new and more dignified ones. This transition can be difficult, because what we have paid attention to etches itself deeply upon our mind, not irrevocably, but in a very real way.

Not long ago, I was trying to talk with my two older sons, Kristoffer and Jonathan, about their day at home during summer vacation. At first, I received the standard reply to the question: "What did you do today?" They answered in unison: "Nothing." I think children are in collusion with each other to raise this ubiquitous phrase whenever parents get "too close" to them and want to share their life. They hope the "intruder" will hear this pathetic response and move on to something more interesting.

Parents usually don't, however. "You mean you sat around all day and did nothing?"

"No, Dad," said Kristoffer. "We watched TV, played a computer game, played baseball outside, and went swimming."

"Wow, that's a lot of nothing," I sarcastically replied. "So what was most interesting about all that?"

They immediately seized upon the movie they had watched on television that morning. In excruciating detail, Kristoffer and Jonathan outlined each frame of the film for me, fighting over who would tell what part when and in how much detail. In the end, I felt like I had watched the film with them.

"What about the other things you did?" I asked.

Silence.

"How was the pool?"

"It was OK," Jonathan said.

I pushed a little more, and then let them alone.

I was amazed at how little they had to say about "real life" events. No great detail was given about the time they spent with their friends at the pool or how the sports activities proceeded. Months later, I recalled this incident with Kristoffer when he asked to watch what Marianne and I deemed an inappropriate movie. He whined, and then let us have it with the heavy guns. "All my friends have seen it already."

Ouch! It became clear that we were the "mean" parents, the uptight, holier-than-thou parents. Maybe we should lighten up, I thought for a moment, and then I remembered the day when the most powerful images inside his head were ones created for him by a filmmaker. After recalling that day for Kris, I asked: "Do you see why we are cautious about what goes into your mind? Look at how vividly every detail of that movie stayed with you. There is great power in the image, and we want your mind filled with positive and dignified stories, not things that are too bloody or negative toward the good things in life."

For one brief moment, I saw in his eyes and face a trace of understanding. He stopped whining, backed down, and went to work on a Lego™ project. Reason had won a small victory.

What goes into our heads and hearts works its way into our thinking and, therefore, into our deciding and choosing. We become what we pay attention to. Patricia Lamoureux reminds us:

In Thomas Aquinas' understanding of the virtues, they are acquired by practicing good deeds that create established habits. As we repeat the actions, habits are deepened and moral character formed. At the same time, just as practice builds up good habits, the lack of practice—or bad habits—destroys virtue. We become just by practicing justice; faithful by persistent acts of fidelity; and honest by telling the truth most of the time. Just as the body is formed by repeated exercise, so too, is character shaped by what we do. Joggers run regularly because they believe it will make them healthier as well as feel and look better. Usually a pattern of running is established that enables the person to engage the experience with more and more ease, less and less effort. It is not expected that running will affect one's personality, appearance, and behavior only during certain times, but that a change occurs over time that will affect all aspects of a runner's life. So, too, it is with character and the virtues. Habits, whether good or bad, become a pattern in our lives that influences attitudes and behaviors in our interpersonal relationships, our work lives, and our societal involvements. ("The Relation of Character and Public Office" in *Josephinum Journal of Theology* n.s. 6:1 [Winter/Spring 1999] 32-33.)

For a moral conversion to be complete, one has to be immersed in a community life that arranges itself according to symbols, images, and activities that are congruent with human dignity. Without such a community, the interior life will be led astray. The interior life develops through growth in virtue *and* through alterations in the external circumstances of our daily lives. This alteration may take some time; we have to be patient with ourselves during conversion because "the world" we previously inhabited made its mark on us partially from the *outside* in.

Meditation Room:
What "worlds" have you left behind
in coming to follow Christ?

I like to hike with my family. On a recent occasion, we chose to hike at a place we had never been before, Conkles Hollow in southern Ohio. Due to the heights the hiking trail reaches,

Marianne decided to stay at home with our infant son, Liam. When we arrived at the park, my boys were immediately impressed with its ancient beauty. After some time exploring the woods, we hit the trail that took us up along the rim of the cliffs.

As we walked along the trail, I tried to be the perfect "PBS Dad" and called attention to interesting trees, geological features, insects, birds, and the deer and fawn that passed in front of us. They acknowledged these things rather cursorily, then continued in their conversation about how great the woods would be for laser tag or what they did on the baseball computer game they played recently at home. I felt rather intrusive pointing things out to them on the hike, and after a while I just let them talk uninterrupted.

When we finally reached the top of the cliffs, we set out on the trail that skirts the precipice and follows an outcropping of rock. It was a dramatic trail, with beautiful views of the valley or "hollow" below. We came to one outcropping and stood motionless looking out over the vista. The boys' conversation stopped, and we sat and looked silently over the cliff's edge for a few moments. "This is cool," they said.

We grew silent again. I said: "Why don't you sit on the outcropping and rest." Immediately, Jonathan and Kristoffer took off their backpacks to use them as pillows on the smooth, table-flat rocks. I continued to gaze outward as the boys laid down to rest. I turned to see them lying in the warm spring sun, and, to my surprise, they had fallen asleep. We had been hiking for a couple of hours by then, and fatigue had overtaken them. It was a beautiful and peaceful sight, to see them asleep on the rocks. I sensed a total trust in them toward God, the creation around them, and me. It was a trust deep enough to give themselves over to the vulnerability of sleep.

I remember this event because, as a metaphor, it highlights a couple of cogent points about conscience formation and moral conversion. When we entered the forest, the boys had set foot in a totally new world for them, and yet, by evidence of the content of their conversation, the effect of their former world was still dominant. I could not instantly crack that world, even with explicit conversation about their immediate surroundings. Their minds were still filled with the fruit of what they had attended to over the last few days. This is true for all of us. Even when we enter the *new* world of discipleship, the *old* world of past loves and preoccupations is still in our minds because of its powerful formation effects.

The longer we stayed in the new world of the woods, my sons' minds slowly began to shift and pay attention to current experience. The boys grew silent at the top of the cliff, looked and cried out how beautiful it was, and finally got to a point where they felt so comfortable within this new world that they could give themselves over to it, trust, and fall asleep.

Moral conversion is akin to this process, as we replace what was superficial in the mind with things of sturdier fare. The old world does not immediately secede, but over time the new environment of faith in God and love for moral goodness etches its beauty within the conscience and silently enters us, to instruct us in moral truth. Perhaps Scripture or the lives of the saints or incidences from life experience overtake us like the forest and cliffs overtook my sons, and we soon find we have given our minds to new things. We begin to think new thoughts and leave behind the less dignified images that currently occupy our minds and hearts, replacing them with the fruit of contemplating the beauty of virtue.

The conscience is simply the mind judging what is morally

right or wrong. It is, however, a mind that has been penetrated and affected by what a person loves. Thus, it is not simply a mind that deduces or judges with cold logic; it is a mind that has focused upon objects that fascinate us, objects that give us pleasure or meaning, and ultimately upon objects or persons or ideas that we come to love. The will chooses what the mind pays attention to, and in this ability is our power to form the conscience.

My sons have part of their minds focused on entertainment, which is certainly not nefarious in itself, but the mind can come to welcome more substantive things to love as well. Coming to realize that our minds can handle sturdier fare signals an interest in an intellectual conversion. After we have had our fill of intellectual junk food, we begin to go searching for richer fare. We begin to ask what it is about life that is really important. Important does not mean serious in the way certain intellectuals think of it; they would have us in the library all day reading nonfiction, and topping the evening off with the *Wall Street Journal*. No, important refers to a philosophical and theological approach toward life that *desires fidelity to goodness*. Moral goodness is certainly not stuffy, uptight, or without a lightness. The most virtuous people I know are simple, to the point, and quick to laugh. There is a joy about following the conscience and developing virtue that is its own reward; it becomes a call to conversion to those who now exist within the shadows of superficiality and vice.

Again, we are called to a moral depth that is not necessarily co-extensive with intellectual depth. Certainly, history has known brilliant persons who have executed immoral activity using cunning and wit, as well as dullards who embarked upon evil in their own right. The universal ingredient for those called to fidelity to the human identity, however, is moral goodness, not a high IQ.

This goodness can be developed within both the wise and the simple.

A friend once remarked that a female student at the college he attended was quite physically beautiful, but he could never imagine dating her because she was an "airhead." After a pause, a second friend said quietly: "But, you know, *I* could see the possibility of getting to know her better because she is such a *good* person."

What is of real value to the human? Over the centuries, beauty has been touted as vital, and intellect as well, but truly it is goodness that is the real value of living. Upon the occasion of our death, who would not rather hear praise for their moral goodness within the eulogy, and not simply comments on their gifted intelligence or physical beauty? Handsome, beautiful, smart, and talented people die everyday, but these attributes do not indicate a morally faithful human life.

In the end, forming the conscience to consistently recognize goodness, and having that conscience present goodness as the only option for behavior, is the definition of a successful life, the good life. If moral goodness, and fidelity to it in the context of faith in God, is the "important" or "serious" point of life, then how do we develop the capacity to listen for moral truth in the voice of conscience?

Meditation Room:

Who is the most virtuous person you have ever known?
What was your primary attraction to his or her way of life?

When one is tempted to do or think things that are against the dignity of human life, these temptations first appear as subtle ideas that seek to be embraced and then acted upon. Entertaining a tempting thought allows it to gather strength, because it is being welcomed as a viable option. For the virtuous person, the next step is to usually abandon the temptation, allowing it to dutifully retreat to the recesses of the mind. It can, however, be summoned back immediately, or it may spontaneously intrude and beckon again. At this point, the virtuous person decides to resist this voice of temptation and attend instead to the voice of truth and goodness.

Each decision is a real choice, and each will have a real effect upon the character of the one who does the choosing. To distinguish vice from virtue is the result of skills developed over time spent at virtue's well. We need to be drenching our minds in virtue through story, worship, prayer. We need specific training of our will, in order to choose the good through prudent, chaste, just, or courageous actions. Eventually, we come to recognize and distinguish legitimate desire from temptation. It is a skill that is developed through example, but it is better and more strongly formed within us if known through both the teaching and witness of others.

During temptation, the conscience will call to the person as well, appearing as ideas to resist the evil proffered by the temptation. It will speak clearly, but the conscience can be drowned out by the inordinate desire of temptation. Temptation makes promises based only upon rationalizations, masking its real motives with seemingly nobler or even pragmatic thinking. Here we are at the heart of moral evil manifesting itself as a lie.

All moral evil presents itself as something it is not, otherwise few would choose it. The skill that Christians need to develop is one that can detect and resist the lies of moral evil masquerading as innocuous pleasure, or even just demands, such as revenge parading as "just punishment." This skill is perfected in a life that actively pursues Christian conscience formation and virtue development through the ordinary circumstances of one's daily life, as explicitly supported by the Church.

Many are fond of pointing out that the temptation to do evil is all around us. We easily point to the popular media and culture as carriers of such temptation. What is not emphasized enough is that the Church, in the form of its members, is all around us as well. The formation of conscience depends upon the connectedness we feel to our faith and to our parish community everyday and in every circumstance. Because many of us do not know how to "be Church" for one another, we are reduced to "waiting" to "go to church." Many people still think of "the Church" as those who are ordained or vowed religious, and will only talk to clergy about a moral problem.

Of course, worship during the week at Mass, prayers before the Blessed Sacrament, and—most especially in Lent—the celebration of the sacrament of reconciliation are all worthy and necessary commitments that should bring us into the church building. More to the point for lay life, however, is a consciousness, which is ever weakening in these secular times, that should bring us to the Church that surrounds us.

Countless numbers of us work in and among the Church every day of our lives, because we work alongside other people of faith. To the left and right of us are brothers and sisters in Christ. One member of the Church could counsel us, pray for us, advise us on Scripture, and even share his or her own struggles with temptation and how he/she overcame them. Another member could bring our needs to their family prayer time and relate deeply to our struggles in the midst of a lay vocation just like his or her own, be he/she single or married.

Meditation Room:

What is the most effective process for you to conquer temptation to sin? Did you ever share this insight, as a gift, with another believer?

The greatest resource for conscience formation and victory over temptation is left fallow for some Christians, because when we are in the church building on Sunday, very little is said about the Church that should "be-a-building" in the secular character and commitments of lay life. This charism of the laity—to be witnesses to the Gospel in the nooks and crannies of culture—is one oriented to fill that same culture with faith, hope, and love. Through this living out of the theological virtues, the laity endeavor to move the culture away from moral evil and toward an eagerness to embrace moral goodness.

The stumbling block for this cultural reformation is that many Catholic Americans embrace the market and political values of privacy, choice, and achievement as their key values for conscience formation. As a result, we are reticent to bother people with our problems, thinking we are duty-bound to preserve a primary cultural value: the sacredness of private lives. Thus privacy becomes even more sacred a value than Christian community. We continue to work alone or set policy alone or seek our own counsel, when many Christians surround us and may be able to help us in our call to moral growth and conversion.

As Catholic Americans, too, we have become so inarticulate about moral teachings that many feel hesitant to speak of these things even for the good of another. We are silent about what is good in order to protect privacy, and because we have lost interest in and the ability to speak a Catholic moral vocabulary. The future of both resistance to temptation and Christian conscience formation depends upon the dissolution of this Catholic conspiracy of silence within the larger American culture. Temptation is always easier to succumb to when we think we are in this life alone and when we have few interior resources upon which to draw.

A friend of mine who is a seminarian had the occasion to be working with a lay ministry student at a diocesan training session. They began talking about their lives and futures. The lay student began to take the seminarian into his confidence and spoke about how he was looking forward to having sex with his girlfriend sometime soon. The seminarian was somewhat shocked, and asked if he was engaged or soon to be married. "No," the man said, "but we love each other."

The seminarian began to speak about the virtue of chastity to the lay ministry student. This student noted that he had never really heard about chastity. How could it be that a lay ministerial student had to be convinced to look again—no, for the first time—at the virtue of chastity? What stories, formative symbols, and doctrines were in his mind? Which ones was he never introduced to?

The parish *as community of faith*—not necessarily a community of pals, and definitely not a gathering of busybodies—is formed around the Eucharist in order that we become good *not by ourselves* but *with* others and *for* others. There is a man in my parish who regularly asks for prayers from the men and women he knows to be the unofficial pray-ers in the parish. They are the ones who attend daily Mass or sit before the Blessed Sacrament in adoration, or perhaps are members of the parish prayer and praise group. He told me that he does not really know them, has never been to their homes for dinner or otherwise socialized with them, but he knows that they are there for him; and they seem to know that too, although no one has ever specified this as their "ministry."

Catechetical instruction and homiletics can also regularly encourage the people to be there for one another on the job, in the home, and at play. The Church is all about being leaven for the culture, and the silence of the laity will add nothing to our ability to become good and recognize the voice of Christ in our consciences if we do not first recognize it in communal companionship, worship, and moral doctrine.

The ancient image of Lent as a time of withdrawal is relevant to the formation of conscience if we perceive that our consciences have been inordinately attached to anemic sources of influence. Christians are called to transform the world of culture, work, and politics according to the truths learned through Christ in the Church. It is a powerful and dignified calling. Lent affords us a good opportunity to repent of those habits, attitudes, or behaviors that reflect a preoccupation with the secular. Thus devoid of the religious, we are then called to eagerly respond to our faith and *imbue the secular with religious and ethical meaning*. To do less than this is to render our baptisms impotent and meaningless.

If Christians do not live out of the power of the Spirit dwelling within them and work for change in the secular culture where needed, our baptisms will simply become initiation rites into a private social club. Lent as a symbol of spring, new life in God, reminds us that faith gained in baptism transcends any purely secular meaning of gathering together in a community called the parish.

CHAPTER FOUR

The Desert of Sin

W ithin the liturgical year of the Church, Lent beckons us to reflect upon our standing before God. It asks us to slow down and take a long, deep look at ourselves in the presence of God. Ultimately, Lent is a very positive season of the year. It moves a person from introspection and acceptance of one's sinfulness toward the renewal and reconciliation offered by Christ on the cross and sealed by his Resurrection. It is anything but a season of wallowing in self-pity. Rather, Lent is a time of looking inside, naming evil, finding new sources of moral formation, and then moving on to a life of graced forgiveness in Christ.

Nothing about Lent is morbid or dark if repentance is embraced in a mentally and emotionally healthy way. Of course, one can fear sin and the loss of intimacy with God that sin brings, but, due to the ministries of the Church, *no one needs to be left in that fear*. In fact, if one is paralyzed by the self-knowledge of sin, it is probably due to some emotional or mental pathology, or simply the person's obstinate will. Through the sacraments, prayers, and disciplines of the Church, all is in place to move one from the perimeter of intimacy with God and Church to its dynamic center. Furthermore, even though everyone appropriates the objective reality of reconciliation at his or her own personal pace, it is possible to begin moral renewal, to not realize the unhappiness of sin as a lasting fate.

Usually, moving from sin to virtue is a conversion appropriated over time. In most cases, we are not to rip ourselves violently away from sin and struggle mightily. We are, instead, to offer ourselves to God in our entirety, inclusive of our present sin and virtue, and pray that God will work within us. In this active cooperation with grace, the change that occurs within our hearts will be more sure; truly we become new creations.

Any moral conversion, if it is to be real, must work its way into our minds and hearts. The conversion we undergo is one that transforms our entire person, and so our thought processes, habits, perceptions, and affections all become realigned to a new way of seeing good and evil. Patience with ourselves, as well as with others who are also in the midst of conversion, becomes the key virtue to cultivate. God knows we are on the right track once we embrace such a conversion, and so being gentle on ourselves is not a sign of laxity or weakness of will, but a sign of wisdom.

Of course, the start of a moral conversion can be dramatic and jumpstart a change, but over the long haul of life, the heart of a person must be fully cooperative; otherwise, the person will not adhere to the moral truth for long. The fourth-century Church father Gregory of Nyssa wrote this about the gradualness of moral conversion, comparing it to the coming of spring.

It is *not* the natural custom of spring to shine forth all at once but there come as preludes of spring the sunbeam gently warming earth's frozen surface, and the bud half hidden beneath the clod, and breezes blowing over the earth so that the fertilizing and generative power of the air penetrates deeply into it. One may see the fresh and tender grass, the return of birds which winter had banished and many such tokens which are rather *signs* of spring than spring itself. (Quoted in Thomas K. Carroll and Thomas Halton, *Liturgical Practices of the Fathers*, Wilmington, DE: Glazier [1988] 278-79; author's emphasis.)

What is happening theologically in our moral conversions is that we are coming to enter and participate in the Paschal Mystery of Jesus Christ. We are, in other words, coming to share in the mystery of salvation as offered to us through Jesus' life, death, and Resurrection. This mystery is symbolically and sacramentally available to us in the worship of the Church. To enter the worship of the Church during Lent is to enter the mystery that will sustain our moral conversions and fasten us securely to virtue. This is true because in entering sacramental worship we are encountering Christ, who is Goodness and Truth. The more we yield to the invitation to go deeper into the Paschal Mystery, the more our perception about reality changes; the more we put on "the mind of Christ" (1 Corinthians 2:16). We begin to think like saints. This change of thinking and loving usually flowers gently over the course of time, like springtime slowly overtaking the winter chill.

Meditation Room:

What are the signs in your daily life
of Christ calling you to holiness?

It very difficult today to find people who feel a horror or sense of fear at their own sinful state. This is both a good thing and a bad thing. It is good because there was a time in the not-so-distant past when some Catholics used the sacrament of reconciliation, for example, in a pathological way. They were too scrupulous about minor sins and expressed a serious lack of trust in the forgiving love of God. That attitude was addressed in some of the pastoral writings and practices following Vatican II, wherein the necessity to "name" sin in "confession" was placed in a wider and more appropriate context, underlining the power of the Mass to reconcile the venial sinner to God.

Unfortunately, along with this more complete vision of how one can be reconciled to God grew the notion that the possibility of being *able* to commit a mortal sin was rare indeed. So we no longer confessed pathologically, but we also came to a point where people very rarely confessed at all, even in a mentally and affectively healthy way.

Fewer people celebrating the sacrament of reconciliation was claimed by some to be proof of our newfound sanity. I wonder about that. The only thing about sin that has lessened in our culture is our skill at naming it. Sin still exists, and its effects are still known within us and in our behavior toward others. What is lacking is our capacity to be *moved* by our own sins in an appropriate manner, and to ask for God's mercy and forgiveness.

There is also a lack of awareness that sin works its way into our hearts through a social or communal conspiracy. If there is a community of virtue in the company we keep, there can just as likely be a community of vice in society and culture. Our private view of sin is evident in these kinds of popular arguments: "If you don't like what is on television, turn it off," or, "If you don't like what a store is selling, don't shop there." Once again we see here an extreme privatism that mirrors our economic minds but not our baptismal identities. Sin is not simply closed within our hearts—it is spilled out of our hearts into culture.

Our call as Christians is to mold culture, to influence society's values, in order that our public lives mirror what is good. Our faith tells us that advancement in moral rectitude is not a matter of living in a cultural wasteland with a pure heart; eventually the wasteland will overwhelm the pure of heart and reconfigure them. Instead, the pure of heart are called to overwhelm the wasteland! We need both hearts of virtue and communities of virtue. Public models of Christian virtue are indispensable to forming future generations of Catholics.

On the other hand, it is also a good thing that we feel less horror at our own sinful state. Many leaders in the Church today received and reveled in the message of the 1970s that God loves us. This is not to conclude that the last generation totally eradicated every individual's insecurity about being loved by God; those involved in pastoral counseling will attest to the fact that many individuals are still plagued by this doubt. There was, however, an *institutional* rediscovery of the love of God by theologians and preachers alike. They counseled persons to stop being so uptight about sin and conscience. "Relax, God loves you." This bumper sticker slogan summarizes very well the message given and received by the '70s generation, which was a response to an excessive legalism in Church life during the previous generation.

Certainly, teaching about God's love is a vital message, central and absolutely core to the Christian faith. The other question, however, that yokes itself to our knowledge of God's love is: Do we love God? As with all love, one proves its presence within the heart through behavior that is faithful to the nature of love. God may love us, and God may forgive us, but soon we come to realize that the Christian faith is not simply about being loved by God—it is also about loving in return. Does our daily behavior reflect our love for God? Being loved is not supposed to be an excuse for "getting away with murder," an attitude we recognize immediately as juvenile. Is each generation fated to be able to grasp only a portion of the truth about God and ourselves? Are we to alternate between unworthy generations, which focus upon the sinful self to the point of excluding God's merciful love, and the other extreme of presumptuous generations, which expect divine love *as a right* no matter what our behavior?

Meditation Room:

What is one of the most significant acts of love toward God that you have done lately?

Obviously these extremes are not universally true of each person in a generation, or we would never have saints present among us. Saints understand the tension correctly and accept the love of God and, in this love, also see clearly their own sin and repent and rejoice in God's mercy. Saints are not a dime a dozen in the parish, but they are there and they do live the truth of the moral doctrine of Catholicism. Like King David, when they repent they ask for forgiveness. We, like them, *can* really learn to *accept* God's love and at the same time *name* our own sin.

Oddly enough, being loved and recognizing our sinfulness go together. Both scrupulosity and presumption can be healed by keeping together these two truths: God loves me, and I am a sinner. Once we start trying to deny that God loves us and that we are "unworthy," or, alternately, that we have no sin because God's compassion does not really take our sinful behavior seriously, the truth of our identity goes awry. We are loved by God, but this divine love is not an accomplice to our rationalizations.

Furthermore, we do sin, but these sins do not exhaust God's love for us like a tired parent who cannot tolerate us any longer. No, when accepted, this divine love moves us to name our sin, and, in that truthful state, to accept the mercy that God offers. In that mercy, we are reconciled to the truth; we stand again as people who are freely loved by God, as forgiven and *really* in need of forgiveness, as persons who acted wrongly but found God to be always and unconditionally "for us" (Romans 8:31).

The polar temptations of denying God's love or presuming it, of denying our ability to sin or wallowing in it unto depression, wreak havoc on any authentic moral conversion. In the sacraments of reconciliation and marriage, and in various spiritualities that form a heart eager to listen, the Church gives us some ways to avoid these extreme temptations.

There is another common disposition regarding sin that has arisen in our present day: the self-deception of rationalizing. Many of us feel we are victims of others' sins but have none of *our own* to name before the priest. Recently, I was speaking with a priest about the growing popularity of cohabitation for engaged Catholic couples. I asked if many of the couples that he prepares for marriage are living together before their vows and, by implication, are having sex. He answered that the majority are. He also commented that the Catholic Church ought to put a moratorium on giving sexual ethical advice for the "next fifty years. No one is listening anyway." I could feel his frustration at trying to teach an ethic that is rejected by the popular American culture. "Just leave the whole sin thing alone," he said. "Look, people aren't persuaded that they need to confess sin; they take care of it privately, through prayer in their hearts. We get nowhere poking around in people's hearts. They are much too complex and too delicate."

A week previous, I had given a lecture at a parish, and a woman came up to me and said: "I like what you had to say about the sacrament of reconciliation, but our priest never posts any public confessional times. I know we are a small parish, but I feel uncomfortable just showing up at his door or calling on the phone to see if he is in. I wish he would just sit in the Church and wait for us to come to celebrate the sacrament. Also, something else, when I do come to him and confess sin, he listens and says the prayers, but oftentimes he says at the end, 'I hope you feel better,' implying that my sins are so small that *he* simply celebrated the sacrament because *I* insisted. I don't think he thinks I really sinned."

So which is it? Do lay people want priests to hear their sins or not? Do priests want to celebrate the sacrament of reconciliation, which admittedly can become tedious? (As one priest friend of mine commented recently: "Humans are not very creative when it comes to sinning.")

Discounting the irrelevant fact that confession may not be very "entertaining" for the priest, it would seem that this sacrament is the symbol of Lent. It was common in the early days of the Church to view the forty days of Lent as a time for growing in virtue and purity of mind. We see that fasting, care for the poor, and confession of sin hold a traditional place in the lenten practices that foster such a development of virtue. Another Church father, Caesarius of Arles, noted the following:

We ought to rest from the winds and the sea of this world by taking refuge in the haven of Lent, and in the quiet of silence to receive the divine lessons in the receptacle of our heart. Let us with all solicitude strive to repair and compose in the little ship of our soul whatever throughout the year has been broken, or destroyed, damaged, or ruined by many storms, that is, by the waves of sins. (Quoted in Carroll and Halton, *Liturgical Practices of the Fathers,* 288.)

Lent becomes that springtime wherein we repair the damage done by a winter of sinful storms that came from our hearts and caused havoc on others and ourselves. The sacrament of reconciliation appears as that sacramental encounter most relevant during Lent in assisting in such repairs. The priest I was speaking with further noted: "Look, no one is coming to confession. We ought to listen to the laity and change this sacrament or incorporate it in a larger vision of forgiveness." Not all laity, however, are staying away from this sacrament, and certainly not all are approaching it with pathological dispositions. Certainly many do not celebrate it anymore, but that does not mean that we ought not catechize parishioners in its power and grace of healing. We have some options, with the rites given to us by the Church, for the celebration of this sacrament; private and communal options should be offered on a regular basis.

All moral conversions have as their end the creation of a pure heart in individuals and the creation of a just society. What is in our hearts is most vital, because from the heart or conscience flows all behavior. Our actions define us up to a point, and they create the culture in which we all now live. Nothing gets built, written, or created that is not first found in the human heart. That is why interior conversion of the heart toward virtue is and has always been the most pressing moral goal for society.

There is a delicate interplay between the development of virtue and the development of a just society. It is one of those "chicken and egg" questions. Which comes first in a just society: the good and virtuous person or the laws needed to establish knowledge of what is good? If it is the law that comes first, however, how do we know a good law from a poor one unless we are guided by virtue? Good people and good societies are created and sustained on many fronts in social life, such as the individual development of virtue, which is enhanced and influenced by civil and religious laws, customs, and traditions.

Meditation Room:

What virtue is most needed today in civil society? in your home? in your heart?

We know that in taking up a virtue one has to let go of a vice. This taking up and letting go is the core movement in the moral conversion of the person. It can be the core movement in social change as well. Think of how a whole society had to let go of vice in the abolition of slavery and legal segregation. Consider how we are still working for that day when our North American society will let go of the vices surrounding the killing of innocent children in utero or the movement toward the killing of innocent sick through euthanasia. Even as we long to be virtuous, and take the pastoral and ethical steps to assure such a goal, we are reminded of how deeply sin gets caught within our character.

The pull of sin will still exist, as a residue within our character, even after we mark our conversions, and so acts of mortification or penitential practices are appropriate during Lent. Traditionally, mortification involves exercises acknowledging that we are chained to our senses in an inordinate way. Oftentimes, we need to *deny* the self its egocentric desires or *take up* charitable acts so that the residue of vice within us might be purified and replaced by a heart ordered to goodness and love.

The idea of sin leaving a residue was underscored for me in a conversation I had with an acquaintance at my parish church. He confided, after a catechetical session, that he struggled with lying. He had lied so often that he was not sure now himself what was true about his day and what was not. The pattern of lying began when he was asked by his boss or a colleague or even his spouse to do something that was inconvenient for him at that time or that was not a priority for him. He would make up some excuse so that he could continue doing whatever he was doing. The excuse was always a lie. He would feign sickness, lie about imaginary business meetings, or simply say he was unavailable. Meanwhile, he sensed that his world was getting smaller and smaller. Everything revolved around him, while others' needs and their legitimate claims upon him went unheeded and unmet. People just thought he was a very busy man, and soon he was left alone to attend to his misguided priorities.

This gnawing sense of isolation began to bother him, and eventually he found himself in counseling, and then celebrating the sacrament of reconciliation. He made a vow not to lie to his wife anymore, and to try to respect her. The "try" part is what is interesting about the residue of sin. In our conversation, he related that he had made that vow to his wife more than six months ago, but it was still a struggle sometimes to say "No" to his personal agenda and to put her first. He had been tempted to lie on several occasions, and a couple of times he did, to excuse himself from something she wanted him to do. "When does all that garbage within us finally get out?" he asked.

It took many years of lying to make that man a liar, and it will take some time to remake himself into one who loves the truth and is not afraid to live it. This is so because of how deeply sin takes root in us. When we cooperate with sin it comes out of us only to "return" to us and create us. Since we freely cooperate with sin, it fills our mind, will, and heart. Disentangling it from the very depths of who we are takes time, and, of course, divine and ecclesial assistance.

Asking for prayer for oneself is always a delicate affair because of its self-revelatory nature, but it is a powerful aid in the movement from sin to virtue. The prayer of the community represents the power of love, and when this power is offered to God for our sake, it becomes a saving force that converts us from sin.

Certainly, one can be discreet about requesting prayers for one's own conversion, but enlisting them seems to be central to conversion. Not only does this unleash the power of divine love, but it also explicitly places us in the context of community, a chief aid given to us by God for our conversion. We are not in this alone. Since the beginning of the Church, it has been acknowledged that persons are to go to a brother or sister in Christ and seek prayer and counsel for conversion from sin (James 5:16). In fact, it was this kind of practice, further developed in Irish monasteries around the sixth century, that formed our present-day understanding of penance and the sacrament of reconciliation.

Intercessory prayer for the conversion of sinners recognizes our intimate communion with one another in Christ. It simultaneously shows our concern for those among us who are personally suffering from their own sin, and it shows concern for the victims of sin as we pray and long for its eradication among us. It is sin that blocks the individual from intimacy with God, and it is sin that blocks the community from showing authentic concern for the common good.

Meditation Room:

When was the last prayer said for you that held recognizable power? When did you last pray for another?

We never get to a point in our lives where we can say we are perfectly virtuous. We always exist *in via*; we are "on the way." The development of virtue is a complex growth in appropriating our own dignity before God and consistently living it out. That does not mean we will always have the right answers for others or ourselves, but we will be headed in the right direction in our love of goodness. The desire to be good is crucial, because it sets the direction of our dispositions and choices. This desire will deepen and become permanent within us the more we choose the morally right thing and the more we pray within the eucharistic liturgy for this desire to become true to our identity.

We can place ourselves at the very heart of salvation as Jesus Christ's self-offering to God the Father is made present sacramentally at each Mass. In this act of worship, we remember—we participate in—the Paschal Mystery. Participation in this sacramental remembrance is most laudatory during the lenten season, as we let go of sin and are taken up into a new life in Christ. Moral conversion will be facilitated for the disciple of Christ in this liturgical act of remembering; God remembers us and we remember God. We are made present to one another so that communion may occur, and this act of remembering is crucial for moral conversion because it keeps us faithful to the truth of who we are.

Scripture tells us that Daniel plainly saw through the idol that the king was worshiping; he laughed at the suggestion that this idol was alive and could, according to the king, even consume a meal. The king was incensed, and set out to prove to Daniel that the idol was alive. The king locked the door of the temple where the idol was kept, and noted that, in the morning, the food that the king placed before this god would be gone, as it was on every occasion. Daniel scoffed at such a claim, inviting the king to believe in the true living God of Israel. The king then placed Daniel's life on the line. He ordered that if the food was not there in the morning, Daniel would be killed; if it was there, the king's own priests would be killed. In the morning the food was gone, but Daniel had seen through the trickery of the priests and pointed out to the king that there were "footprints of men and women and children" on the floor of the temple (Daniel 14:20).

The king seized the priests and killed them for deceiving him. Daniel destroyed the idol, and the king eventually came to worship Daniel's God. The people, however, were frightened that their idol had been destroyed. They convinced the fainthearted king that Daniel should die, and so he was thrown to the lions to be eaten. Through a miracle, the lions did not kill Daniel, the prophet Habakkuk fed him, and Daniel rejoiced: "You have remembered me, O God, and have not forsaken those who love you" (Daniel 14:38).

The story of Daniel instructs us in the ways of fidelity to God. The writer wanted us to know that when we stay faithful to God, we will know God's fidelity to us. Remembering the faithfulness of God to us personally, and/or to the Church, gives us strength to go forward toward intimacy with God in moral faithfulness. Our faith will be tested, but *when we remain faithful*, we will ultimately know the fidelity *of God* toward us.

God does not abandon us. God remembers us, and we remember God's faithfulness to the Covenant. As Daniel was saved by God's hand and fed by his prophet, so grace and the Word guard us in our efforts to grow in virtue. God's presence is with us, and we can encounter God in the meal of remembrance, the Eucharist. Truly, the Eucharist is our food of fidelity. As Daniel was given bread to keep up his strength in the face of rejection and the threat of death, so we are given the food of fidelity and hope in the Bread of Life, in the very mystery of salvation in sacramental form. If we feed on this bread, our hearts and our consciences will feed on truth itself, the very person of Christ. Through this meal, we will be given the strength and the courage to follow Christ's commands and show our love for him as he taught:

"If you love me, you will keep my commandments. And I will ask the Father, and he will give you another Advocate, to be with you forever. This is the Spirit of truth....They who have my commandments and keep them are those who love me; and those who love me will be loved by my Father, and I will love them and reveal myself to them" (John 14:15-17a,21).

Listening to Christ in love, through his commands, unifies the believer with God. This is, of course, the ultimate goal of Christianity and our personal goal in moral conversion. The commands of Christ are firm norms that prevent us from hurdling toward a life of infidelity to our baptismal identity. We are to move from moral evil to the grace-filled life by cooperating with the truth of baptism. Lent affords us the opportunity to delve more deeply into that truth. In the baptized life, we consciously embrace our unity with Christ in everything we do. Baptism brings us into communion with the very "life blood" of God in Christ, and without that communion our soul withers and dies, as Jesus said plainly:

> I am the vine, you are the branches. Those who abide in me and I in them bear much fruit, because apart from me you can do nothing....If you keep my commandments, you will abide in my love, just as I have kept my Father's commandments and abide in his love" (John 15:5,10).

In Christ, we are reborn and sustained in the life of the Spirit. Each Lent, the Church offers us the opportunity to reappropriate that birth and deepen that sustenance through repentance. Baptism, Lent, and the new life of springtime all cooperate in the Christian imagination and liturgy to turn our heads and hearts from sin toward the fountain of grace in Christ. This grace, which is the person of Christ himself, appears before us not simply with an invitation, but his very presence in our lives places a *demand* upon our conscience. Is he or is he not the very embodiment of God's salvation? That is the dramatic "Yes" or "No" answer to the question about Christ's very being (Matthew 16:13). The lenten call is this: If we love Christ, we will listen to him. The person and the message of Christ become one—one unified opportunity for persons to respond to who they are in God. In this response is our dignity and destiny.

This offer of salvation in Christ is exactly what the reality of grace means: a pure gift. In this call from God in Christ to come into union with him, we find that God is offering us a new life, a new kind of living. It is a transcendent living, a life that is not simply natural with some added transcendental meaning, but one that has been lifted up in and through the natural to the supernatural. We indeed have been born again.

It is through baptism that the rebirth objectively occurs, and we spend the rest of our lives *living into* that truth by means of many large and small conversions or awakenings. We awaken to who we are in Christ, and that insight fuels our choices and dispositions. Over the years of living, we are called to share in the dying and rising of Christ as we die to personal sin and rise with Christ to share his holiness.

Life in Christ is not simply to serve the moral life, but is incorporated into the mystery of redemption as well. By this it is meant that our character and conscience participate in the saving works of Jesus, thus unleashing upon society tangible evidence of the communion of saints. The Christian strives to stay one with Christ and, by doing so, influences society with moral behavior and/or a testimony of hope through the forgiveness of sins.

Through the indwelling of the Spirit given at baptism, we are connected to Christ from within the very depths of our own spirit. Nothing can separate us from the love of God (Romans 8:35-39). Christ calls to us from the very depths of our spirit, through our mind. Thus is Christian conscience born. We who are baptized no longer simply *think about* right and wrong; we think about it *out of love for Christ*. This is different from simply thinking ethically, as one may do in a court case or in a university ethics class. The latter two use only philosophical or legal categories of thought. The Christian conscience operates out of a personal dialogue between oneself and Christ—a dialogue that occurs at the heart of one's search for truth within the community of the Church.

A Christian is one who communicates interiorly with the Spirit of Christ in the midst of a community of like believers. This interior conversation is then enfleshed in an ethic and in forms of worship. The ethic and forms of worship then work in reverse, further deepening the interior conversation through repeated behavior, ritual, symbol, and narrative. In other words, the morally good Christian lives out of faith, out of a trusting and deep relationship with the living God in Christ. We take on "the mind of Christ" over the years, just as a husband and wife take on each other's mind and virtues over many years of marriage. In deep unity with Christ by the power of the Spirit in baptism, Christians grow to think like Christ; they thus become sanctified, holy, saints. The key to Christian moral conversion is to stop being anxious about being formed in Christ, and alternately to let Christ be formed in us through participation in the life of the Church (Galatians 2:19-20).

The gift of Lent is that we are invited to slow down and take a look at ourselves before God—then to name our sin, ask for God's mercy and forgiveness, and enjoy a spiritual and moral rebirth rooted in God's love. In coming to share in the Paschal Mystery of Christ, we gradually cooperate more and more with God's grace; we leave behind the residue of sin and live creatively in the tension between our sin and God's love for us. Lent, and the sacrament of reconciliation, help us do this; they help us to remember God's fidelity to us despite our sin.

CHAPTER FIVE

Leaving the Desert

Celebrating the sacrament of reconciliation is, for many Catholics, a most daunting prospect. This sacrament has been the source of many jokes, composed perhaps by persons seeking to reduce the level of stress they feel regarding one of its main components: naming personal sin.

The naming of one's own sin to oneself and to a priest is self-revelatory to the point of evoking anxiety. Initially, it can be true that some level of apprehension may accompany this sacrament, but over time, with regular celebration of this form of worship, anxiety diminishes. Most positively, the sacrament of reconciliation promotes truthful self-knowledge regarding sin *in the context of Christ's saving presence*. Once someone experiences both the naming of sin and the reception of God's mercy in this sacrament, he or she actually begins to *celebrate* this sacrament and see it as a great gift from Christ and his Church.

I remember the day that my attitude toward reconciliation changed forever. I had made my way to the parish church, and waited outside the reconciliation room, in prayer, with a number of other parishioners. Soon, it was my turn to enter the room and celebrate the sacrament. The priest and I went through the rite as usual. When he finished the prayer of absolution and gave me my penance, I got up and walked toward the door. He stopped me, as I was leaving, to say: "Remember, when you leave here it is as if you have been born again!"

No priest had ever said that to me before. On that day, the actuality of the renewing grace of God through penance came clearly to my mind and heart. I felt enveloped in the mercy of God—the God of second chances, the God who always does something new (Isaiah 43:19). I left the reconciliation room and entered the nave of the church with a deep and quiet joy. It is that joy which I now associate with this marvelous sacrament.

Meditation Room:

Recall a time when you experienced
reconciliation with a friend or family member.
What was the source of your joy?
What aspects of this reunion are relevant
to how one comes to be reconciled with God?

In order to see why penance can be an occasion for joy rather than anxiety, it is helpful to understand the nature of God's mercy. It will be our absolute trust in God's mercy that will facilitate our joyful embracing of this sacrament. Divine mercy is the form God's love takes when this love encounters a repentant sinner. (See John Paul II, *Dives in Misericordia* ["Rich in Mercy"], Washington, DC: United States Catholic Conference [USCC], 1981.)

Mercy is the way of God's eternal existence. Through the revelation of God, which is the life of Christ, we come to know that God's will is the salvation of all persons. The divine mercy shown by God to sinners is not capricious, but constitutes the very life of God. God is Love. God is Salvation. To accept this truth about God's identity prepares us to embrace more fully—through faith, hope, and love—the fact that God ultimately wants communion with us. Sin—those acts and dispositions that weaken or destroy our communion with God—is to be named so that it no longer has power over us. In the sacrament of reconciliation, we give over the power of forming our identities—to the one who truly cares about us and truly has the power to lead us into our deepest dignity: Jesus Christ. As theologian Frederick Buechner said: "The judge will be Christ. In other words, the one who judges us most finally will be the one who loves us most fully" (*Wishful Thinking: A Theological ABC*, San Francisco: HarperCollins [1973] 48).

We name our sins in the presence of the minister of God's mercy so that we may appropriate that mercy and be formed by *God's love* rather than the by *disordered loves* of our sins. In one way, the sacrament of reconciliation is an "identity adjustment" encounter. On the day I've recounted, I entered this sacrament having previously given myself to false or less noble loves, such as the exclusive desires of my ego, only to have the sacrament reintroduce me to our only worthy, ultimate love: God.

Meditation Room:

Whom do you listen to in an effort to form and adhere to moral values? Why are these people or sources trustworthy? How did you decide that they were?

I remember talking with a recent convert to Catholicism about the sacrament of reconciliation. He was sharing his fears over having to actually utter words that described his sin. It was too specific for him; it was too "unnatural." He had been reared in a religious tradition that taught that only a general sorrow for sin was necessary to receive God's forgiveness.

Without denying that in extraordinary circumstances forgiveness for serious sin can be bestowed as a result of "general sorrow," the ordinary route to celebrate the mercy of God for Catholics is to sacramentally name the actual sin. This specificity frightened him. It was the actual naming of the truth about himself that he just could not manage. We talked for awhile, and we soon hit upon a concept that helped him a great deal. This concept was the simple Christian doctrine that Christ is "the way, and the truth, and the life" (John 14:6). If Christ is the truth, we do not have to be afraid to speak the truth about ourselves in his presence. This is so because the truth (Christ) loves us. (See "Declaration on Religious Liberty" 14 in *Vatican Council II: The Sixteen Basic Documents*.)

Meditation Room:

"'You will know the truth, and the truth will make you free.'
These words contain both a fundamental requirement
and a warning: the requirement of an honest relationship
with regard to truth as a condition for authentic freedom,
and the warning to avoid every kind of illusory freedom...
every freedom that fails to enter into the whole truth."
(John Paul II, *Redemptor Hominis*, USCC [1979] 36.)
Recall a time when your confrontation
with truth set you free.

So much of the reticence people feel about approaching the sacrament of reconciliation is contained within this very real requirement of facing and then naming the truth about themselves. The hope and joy of Catholic repentance, however, is that when we name the truth about ourselves, even the darkest truth, Jesus Christ—Truth itself—is present to receive us. In this sacrament, our truths meet Truth itself, who is Mercy. When we name our sins in truth, they are met with divine mercy. The result of this naming is not condemnation, but reconciliation and salvation.

Perhaps we are so used to experiencing personal rejection when speaking the truth to others that we cannot trust that Christ will simply heal our sins in his grace and not use them against us. In the story of the woman caught in adultery, Jesus delivered to her only one deceptively simple command: "Do not sin again" (John 8:11). Jesus' gentleness in this case expresses his mighty divinity in our midst; God can bear our sins, but God knows we cannot! Christ did not have to rant and rave against the woman's sin, because his compassionate presence prepared her to receive in peace the truth about herself. He asks us to stop sinning, to stop living lives that obscure our dignity as the images of God that we are (Genesis 1:26). Instead, we are invited to cooperate with grace, to come to know God and so be morally transfigured.

The Catholic moral life is ultimately about knowing Christ and having communion with him. Having communion with Christ means that we open our minds and hearts to be affected by the Truth that he is and the truths that he teaches. In other words, we have communion with Christ when we allow him to save us from our sin! Augustine DiNoia once wrote: "The ultimate aim of a morally upright life is not so much to please God by successfully living the commandments as to render us fit for the eternal company of the Triune God" (*Veritatis Splendor and the Renewal of*

Moral Theology, eds. Augustine DiNoia, OP and Romanus Cessario, OP, Huntington: IN, Our Sunday Visitor Press [1999] 2). That is where the morally good life leads: to the company of God, both now and forever.

Meditation Room:

How is sharing the company of the most virtuous person you know like a small hint of life in heaven?

The path to heaven crosses right through the sacrament of reconciliation, not as a ritualistic requirement but as a moment of personal awakening regarding one's relation to God and moral goodness. The sacrament stands as a gift from Christ, through the Church, for the necessary discipline of naming sin in an environment of grace. In so naming sin, we can move forward in our life of virtue, the only kind of life that can exist forever in God. This salvation from sin is, of course, sheer gift, and the desire for union with Christ and the consequent sacramental naming of our sins simply expresses our cooperation in freedom with saving grace. It is grace—God's abiding presence with us in Christ—that reaches out to us to soften our hearts and move us to moral conversion.

I once knew a man whose marriage was in deep trouble. It was falling apart due to much self-centered behavior on the part of both husband and wife. He had mentioned to me his dismay over the impending destruction of his marriage and asked me, along with some other persons he was sharing his story with, for prayers.

Three months later I saw him again, and he asked to speak with me. He was very excited and happy. In reporting to me that his marriage was now on the mend, he related the cause for its renewal: "One day, I was working at my desk and suddenly looked up at a picture of my wife and me. I don't know why. All I noticed in looking up was that picture, and all I felt was that we needed to be together as we were in the photograph. I got up from my desk and left work and went to find my wife at her job. I arrived at her workplace carrying flowers and knocked on her door. She opened it, and looked half-astonished and half-skeptical. All I could say was, 'I miss you.'"

He went on to relate that it took many months of hard work and self-denial to begin again to serve one another's good as husband and wife. He told me how hopeful he was for the future. I can only think that it was grace which led that husband to look upon the photo with the disposition that he did. He was moved to sorrow, to action, and then to reconciliation.

It is sin that separates us and maintains divisions between individuals, like my friend and his wife, and even between larger groups, such as nations. All sin, however, whether it remains between two persons or spills out to affect the social order, passes through the human heart. There are no magic formulas for coming to an awareness of our need for reconciliation with God and others, but the Church and its traditions, customs, liturgies, catechesis, and opportunities for service to the poor, can dispose us to await the movement of God within our souls. It is a movement leading to repentance. All sin needs to be personally repented of so that peace may again be present, signaling that those things which separated us from others and from God are now mended.

Individual conversion and repentance are necessary, because actual sin only appears through the free and knowing acts of persons. Since sin begins in us, we need to recognize it as ours, name it, and repent of its destructive effects. To repent of sin implies not simply a turning *away* from evil but also a turning *toward* something good. The gospel tells us to "repent, and believe in the good news" (Mark 1:15). The twin movements of repentance, a turning away from sin, and believing, a turning in trust toward God, make up the full meaning of moral conversion. In this turning we leave behind the false or incomplete values out of which we have lived, and we begin to gain confidence in doing what is right by trusting in the abiding, merciful presence of God in our lives. Through trust in God, we slowly relinquish the need to find solace, pleasure, or diversion in sin, and instead long for the fullness of human dignity in lives lived as children of God. This "turning from" and "moving toward" can be initiated quickly or slowly in a person's life. What is universal, however, is the need to be gentle with one's self once conversion has begun.

During the early stages of moral conversion, we will experience what can be referred to as the "residue" of sin. This residue may manifest itself in bad memories or in stirred up desires for activities that we *thought* we had renounced in the light of faith. This residue of sin should not discourage us or make us think that our conversion was not real; the residue is simply a sign of how deeply sin had attached itself to our character. It has, so to speak, gotten into our bones. Now, in our turning toward Christ, we want his grace to guide us and free us from even the memories of sin, so as to blunt our desire to sin again. We want God's merciful Spirit to dwell within us, to direct our behavior in the light of truth, and to purify us from behavior driven by neediness, obsession, or disordered desire.

It is repentance that assists us in the transition from sin to life in Christ. The great gift of the sacrament is that within its prayers and ministerial presence we sacramentally encounter the living Christ. This encounter strengthens, heals, and directs us away from past desires and toward a life of virtue. This sacrament is, as are all sacraments, a celebration of the living relationship God in Christ has with us. The sacrament of reconciliation can aid in our moral conversion because it is, very simply, the place we meet Christ with an honest conscience and a repentant heart. In regularly coming before Christ in this sacramental way, we practice a humility and a vulnerability that gives Christ deeper and deeper access to our soul. The end result is that the sinful inclinations are replaced with dispositions representative of the "mind of Christ," not the disordered desires of our selfishness or self-hate.

Meditation Room:

Recall a time when you felt Christ most alive in your life. Name the fruits of that personal encounter.

In one of the prayers of contrition provided in the Rite of Penance, we read this:

Father of mercy, like the prodigal son, I return to you and say: 'I have sinned against you and am no longer worthy to be called your son.' Christ Jesus, Savior of the world, I pray with the repentant thief, to whom you promised paradise: 'Lord, remember me in your kingdom.' Holy Spirit, fountain of love, I call on you with trust: 'Purify my heart, and help me to walk as a child of the light.' (*The Rites of the Catholic Church*, NY: Pueblo Publishing [1976] 382.)

What is key in this prayer, and in the whole reality of repentance as a means for moral conversion, is the notion of purity of heart. The heart is the deepest center of personal existence. It is the place where what is true and loving in life claims our allegiance. To be pure of heart is to be a person who loves and desires what is morally good. Our hearts become so centered upon objects worthy of love that we become rightly sensitive to the ill effects of immorality and reject evil with more and more regularity. Over time, as we gradually learn to love this way, evil has less and less power over us. This is so because we have given our hearts over to the God of goodness itself.

Meditation Room:

What are your first reactions to the word "pure"?
How would you apply growth in purity to your moral life?
What kinds of actions and dispositions
would a morally pure person let go of,
and what kinds of actions would be embraced?

An analogy will help to further our understanding of purity of heart. I have a friend who had the practice of dating many women at one time. Most of the time, the women did not know that he was having simultaneous relationships with others. For a variety of reasons, he began to question this kind of dating, and at one point confessed to me that perhaps what he was doing was "not fair." He did, however, keep this dating game going for sometime after this admission.

He then met the woman who was to become his future wife. Suddenly, he did not know what to do. He sought counsel from friends, and even from a professional counselor with whom he was acquainted. "What is happening here?" he wondered. He felt different, desired a different pattern of relating to the women in his life, and began to think that he wanted to narrow his many girlfriends to simply this one woman.

One day, he made the decision to simply concentrate upon her, and soon his heart became configured to hers and formed by his concentrated attention upon her in love. They married after two years of exclusive dating. As he was looking forward to his wedding day, he related to me how different his life was, and how happy and peaceful his heart had become since he had begun to "focus purely, simply, and only upon Margaret."

This is purity of heart in the moral life: to focus purely, simply, and only upon loving the moral good. Of course, it is very difficult to love *a concept* like the moral good. In Christianity, however, we do not have to love an abstract concept; instead, we are called to love the person of God in Christ. This is very concrete, and Christ's presence is mediated universally through so many facets of creation, revelation, and ecclesial life that we are never far from him. Most profoundly, God dwells within the very heart that God is purifying: our own.

In the end, conversion from sin is about what we love, not simply about behaviors to avoid. Christ, the beloved one, leads us to behavior that is faithful to the dignity of our relationship with him, just as my friend's love for Margaret led him to behavior that was befitting marriage.

The sacrament of reconciliation finally results in a life of purity of heart. The discipline of truthfully naming sin, and the comfort and joy of receiving divine mercy, scours our heart and ultimately reconciles the heart to its origin: the Pure One, God.

Meditation Room:

Reflect upon your day today
and note what your heart was really attached to.
What did you pay the most attention to today, and why?
Does the desire for heaven and communion with God
ever contribute to your motivations for being morally good?
How is being good related to being a disciple
of the Savior, Christ?

CHAPTER SIX

The Oasis of Lent

M oral conversion occurs in ordinary experience when we hit a wall or break through one. In other words, moral conversion can be ignited when we reach our limits and experience failure or finitude, or it can be ushered in when we transcend our limits and go beyond the self. We transcend the self by falling in love and/or following the prompting of conscience at the cost of our own ego.

The traditional disciplines of Lent—prayer, fasting, and almsgiving, as well as communal worship—aim at fostering or preparing a person to welcome such limiting or breakthrough experiences. Most importantly, we are prepared *to receive* the truths known in these experiences, since we can rarely, if ever, orchestrate them. More than likely, we are taken up into such experiences, and our preparation beforehand can enhance our acceptance of the truths they carry. What kind of preparation for moral conversion is enfolded within the disciplines of Lent?

Prayer

Saint Teresa Benedicta of the Cross (Edith Stein) once visited a church, before her conversion to Catholicism, and saw a woman alone in prayer before the high altar. Stein had the image of this solitary prayerful woman burned into her religious imagination, and came to see it as a grace from God moving her to conversion. She was very used to seeing people pray at *public* worship services, but that woman before her modeled an intimacy for Edith that each one of us can achieve with God in prayer.

We oftentimes assume knowledge of prayer because it is so basic and universal in the role it plays in the Christian life. As with all things basic, however, we can come to take the presence of prayer for granted and thus lose out on a deeper appreciation for its power and necessity. The first thing to note about prayer that prepares us for moral conversion is its relation to both contemplation and petition. In contemplation, we are gifted with a sense of God's intimate presence in our lives. We are taken into the presence of God in Christ, through the Spirit. At its deepest level, we share in the very prayer of Christ before the Father.

In this kind of prayer, we long to be in the presence of God; we simply want to be with God for no other reason than the fact that we love God. In this way, contemplation is both a task and a gift. As a *gift*, this kind of prayer, even in its *initial stirring desires*, is itself already a sign from God that we are called to the divine presence. To have the desire to be with God is the nascent call to moral conversion, because only the virtuous and grace-filled person can stand in the presence of holiness.

By noting the desire to pray at a deeper level, one is acknowledging the call to become holy, and holiness is simply moral goodness infused with grace. The first prayer of petition we offer, therefore, ought to be one asking for the grace to desire to be in the very presence of God: "O God, please stir deeply within me and call me to yourself for prayer and conversion." Of course, if we have the desire to pray this prayer, we are already touched by

God. God has already found us and is stirring us to desire God's self from *within* our very petition.

We are literally soaking in the presence of God; we are God's images upon Earth (Genesis 2). We are surrounded by a conspiracy of grace, but we ask God for the grace to be in the divine presence because we are not yet perfectly aligned with moral goodness and holiness. We ask God to come close to us so that, in fact, *we* may come close to God, that we may become vulnerable to grace and therefore begin to cooperate with it in our own moral conversion.

Wanting to be in the presence of God has its analogies in human experience, with similar life-altering effects. The most powerful examples reside in domestic life: the desire of a husband to be with his wife and of a wife to be with her husband; the desire of parents to simply "be" family, to be together with their children. These desires are the hidden energy behind holidays. They are special days to be with God, family, and loved ones. It was this energy that partly fueled older conceptions of Sunday as the day of "resting" in relationships, both human and divine.

This is not to say that we always experience the *fulfillment* of these desires when we are with family, however. The weeds of sin and human finitude are regularly mixing with the wheat of God's grace (Matthew 13:24-30). When openness to another's presence does reach fruition in some kind of union, it is a true gift, and deeply satisfying to the human spirit. This union is, in fact, the hope of Christians, in that we are made for such rest in the presence of love itself: God.

The *task* element of prayer is traditionally known in the preparatory stages of prayer. It takes some preparation, "fasting," and self*ish*-denial to ready ourselves to be cognizant of the presence of God all around us. This preparation is measured not in moments or days, but in years and, in fact, becomes the very substance of our lives. The Church is not about the denial of self in Catholic moral living, but is aiming to purify selfishness. In fact, the denial of *selfish* living brings the self to completion.

In the end, the practice of curbing selfishness is always positive. The act of fasting, which can take many forms—from going without food to denial of superfluous pleasures to positive acts of service for others—is the effort to clear from view all that is not of God. In this way, when God seeks to communicate the divine to us, we will not be unduly attached to objects of lesser worth but will readily recognize God's voice and listen to its wisdom. "Unless we have long since held [moral truth] in our hearts by love," we may be prevented from recognizing it as such when it claims our conscience (Aelred Graham, *The Love of God*, NY: Image Books [1959] 222).

The story of Christ walking on the water (Matthew 14:22-33) lends itself to an apt meditation upon the meaning of lenten prayer. Christian life is truly one of learning how to walk on water. It is a commitment to trust in Christ, even if what is being asked or presented looks like the road to suffering or disaster. This is not to say that the Christian life is absurd, or that it asks us to do irrational things. It does, however, ask us to trust in God even when it appears that commitment and trust is impossible. Faith in God is a "trust walk" that demands clinging to the promises of Christ. Faith invites us to yield the self over to God at the point of our greatest vulnerability, our fear of failure, loss, control, and death.

Throughout the Scriptures, Jesus reassures us that he is with us in this call to give up the self; that fear ought not to overwhelm us or tempt us to rely merely on our own resources (Matthew 14:27; Luke 12:32ff). As we are invited to "walk on water" with Christ, we are prepared to respond to such an invitation through the hours and hours we have spent in conversation with God in prayer. Peter got out of the boat and walked toward Christ on the water only because he really knew this Savior and trusted in him deeply. He had come to see that Christ was master over chaos (Matthew 8:23) and, by his word, that which was most terrible could be calmed. We yearn to know this power of Christ as well.

Many people live upon storm-tossed waters for years, bearing illness, rejection, poverty, and more. We hope with Peter, and watch for the day when Jesus will call us out and calm the waters around us, the day when we will feel his hand snatch us from the sufferings of life and we come to rest in his divine love.

Prayer is not a pious act or a devout practice for the sentimental; it truly is the very giving of the self over to Christ. In this giving, we come to know Christ and to prepare for the day when we will be invited to walk on water *in faith*. Ultimately, that is the day of our death, but we undergo many deaths throughout our discipleship as the ego is pared down to size. Whatever our situation, however burdensome or seemingly irrational, we are called in faith to abide with it in prayer. We are to listen closely for Christ calling out to us in the midst of chaos, and offering us his presence as the calm center in the storm of our sufferings. Beyond the struggles of circumstance and limit, we are summoned to rid ourselves of those sufferings that are self-imposed by sin.

The story of Christ walking on the water reminds us to fast from temptations that clamor like waves for our attention and to focus only in faith on the presence of Christ. As Peter looked away from Jesus and sank, seeing foreboding waves, so we too can succumb to the turbulent call of sin. Having trained our hearts to hear the voice of Christ in prayer, we can come to recognize his voice even in the midst of storms, in chaos and temptation and the darkness of not knowing what is to become of a present struggle or difficult situation. Prayer in Lent, and throughout the year, trains us to hear Jesus' voice—to know it, trust it, and hope in it alone in the midst of suffering. In this manner, truly mature Christians can be "fools for the sake of Christ" (1 Corinthians 4:10).

The habit of being able to hear the voice of Christ in prayer is also the virtue needed to obey one's conscience. In times of temptation to sin, we need to be sure that the voices clamoring for our attention are truly of *the* Spirit and not simply any spirit. We need to discern the voices, distinguishing between what is truly for our benefit and what is only a word uttered for our destruction. As the story of Jesus walking on the water testifies, this discerning ability is not always easy. Was Peter killing himself by leaving the boat, or was he simply about to kill his own selfishness and need for control? Each one of us will face similar tests of our ability to recognize Christ's voice within our conscience, as a sea of voices and feelings surround us and beckon us.

The saints of the Church knew of the importance of prayer as a way of life, leading to peaceful consciences that are easily familiar with the real voice of truth. This is the great grace of prayer: Over time we come to know our Lord's voice and even become eager to hear it within the depths of our conscience. For the Christian, living a moral life is not an "obligation"; the more deeply we love the sound of the voice of truth—Jesus—the more we come to see moral living as an easy yoke, a light burden (Matthew 11:30).

This transformation is a paradox, however, because the moral life does not simply become "light"; it still retains a weight to it.

As sinful persons, we still feel the lure of sin, and even though we come to take on "the mind of Christ," we are often still tempted to sink within the waters of that sin. Nevertheless, in becoming good and holy, we do know that hope is now our life. We know where to bring our desires for sin, our feelings of weakness, and our drive for control and misdirected power. As hope-filled persons, we know that we can *trust* more in the promises of Christ to save us rather than *fear* the regular invitations to sin that may intrude upon on our daily lives.

What we aim for in the disciplines of Lent is the purification of our desires, not their eradication. The warped desires that encompass the satisfaction of selfishness or the descent into self-hate remain the focus of Christ's purifying Spirit. Desire is the seed of love, so it needs only to be watered from fresh, life-giving sources, not dammed up entirely. In the end, our purified desires are conveyances for union with what is good and holy, as we aim to be friends with Christ through grace. In this way, we come to love virtue together with Christ. It is this love that constitutes one of our deepest bonds with him. It is a bond cemented in prayer.

Meditation Room:

"One must not forget that the prayer of the individual
relies on the community which it serves,
and that the only ultimate meaning of community prayer
is to lead the individual to God"(Karl Rahner).
Within which setting is your prayer most fruitful:
alone? within a group? with a friend?

Fasting

Recently, I read an advertisement in a newspaper that heralded the arrival of a particular restaurant's new "giant"-sized drink and lunch. Free "giant" refills were offered, too. Soon after, while eating lunch in a local restaurant, I was given a piece of lasagna that was over one-half foot long and almost as deep. Moreover, restaurant buffets are everywhere today in our culture, wherein we can visit the abundantly-supplied table as often as we like. Our society does not appear to be in the mood to fast.

To fast is to deny oneself a certain good thing, because ultimately one desires to be filled, not by that food or drink, but by the Spirit of Christ. As we've seen, our sinfulness can corrupt our hearts and lead us not to love God, but rather to attend to created goods. Fasting is simply a way to discipline and remind the self that it can go astray, trusting more in the consumption of immediately available food and drink than in the promises of Christ.

The poor, however, mostly wrestle with a lack of food and drink, and so spiritually they are often called to heroic hope in the face of their sufferings. Their spiritual discipline is not fasting, per se, but, more immediately, hoping. As a full stomach can cloud over the reality of God's *providence* for the ungrateful wealthy, despair and depression can cloud the reality of God's *presence* with the poor. Food is not an accidental feature of our life; it is a necessity, and we have a right to it. Fasting from food may lead one to open a space for charity to the poor or to clear a place within one's self for welcoming God in prayer.

Ultimately, fasting liberates us from undue self-concern and worry. Jesus chided his followers for being too concerned about what they were to eat, and instead spoke words of trust in the providence of the Father (Matthew 6:31). Christ promised that our *needs* would be fulfilled, not our every want or desire. I have often found that when I fast from meat, it is then that I have the greatest craving for it. Then the desire to eat such food preoccupies my mind. I begin to look forward to the time when I can eat a steak again. I feel resentment for the fast. Consequently, I feel the lack of discipline within me. I experience slight anger. I rationalize. I am tempted to forego the fast. I can, eventually, come to see that I am *too* attached to food. In coming to this conclusion, I can see that fasting has done its job.

What could fill the space of this desire for food other than my craving for the pleasure of eating it? The masters of the spiritual life have always answered that question in two ways: God and serving the needs of others. Fasting can discipline us to pray and learn the ways of charity. It is a means for forgetting the selfish self and further purifying our identity as persons who are loved by God and enabled to love others.

Of course, we do not have to fast simply from food. We can fast or abstain from anything that tempts us to give it undue attention: shopping, television, work, gossip, etc. Sometimes we fill our lives with so much food, activity, or recreation simply because we are afraid of the silences, of the "down time." Other times, it is because we are bored that we turn to excess food or drink. In many cases, our society pushes food upon us like it pushes sex. The lustful images and dialogue that fill the advertising on TV and in magazines conspire to raise our levels of hunger. We respond to these images even if we have just eaten and are satiated. How many times have we been perfectly satisfied with the dinner we had, but a television commercial comes on and we find ourselves stealing out to the kitchen or ordering a pizza? This is not some grave moral evil, per se. This kind of spontaneity can even be fun, but in repeated patterns it is simply an indication of our lack of self-discipline.

A further point about fasting: Jesus is clear that fasting is *not* to be a public display that draws the attention of others (Matthew 6:16-18). Fasting is to be done in private; it is something, in a sense, that is between us and God. Practically speaking, a whole family can fast, so others will know about one's fasting, but only *within* the family. We do not have tell everyone in the neighborhood or the parish that we are fasting. When we keep it private, it becomes an act offered for some intention or some aspect of moral conversion that is needed for the family. A family fast will also be sensitive to the age and spiritual needs of its members, thus mindful of not imposing unjust burdens upon the young, elderly, or infirm.

Our most urgent call to fasting, however, is the call from God to fast from sin. We are creatures of developed habits. We can also come to reject the vices we have developed, and begin instead to develop virtue. Ultimately, we do not want to simply *fast* from sin—we want to *overcome* it in grace. There are sinful activities that we used to do, but with which we no longer struggle. In order to live in hope, it is good to remember the sins we have overcome; any *present* struggle over certain sins can someday be banished to our past as well.

This Lent, perhaps we could choose a habitual sin from which we wish to fast, and so prepare ourselves for the day when that sin will no longer rule over us. That day could very well be Easter Sunday morning. An authentic moral conversion begins with the realization that certain interior attitudes and consequent actions are not in accord with our dignity as the beloved of God. We come to see that life cannot go on as usual, that a transformation is warranted. Many times, with small incremental steps, we cast off sin. Even if there is some backsliding, we never despair, because the journey away from this particular vice has begun, and we know "the one who began a good work among you will bring it to completion" (Philippians 1:6).

If we use the analogy of fasting from sin during Lent as our guide, it could very well be that, this Lent, we begin to turn the corner on certain immoral behaviors that have been plaguing us for sometime—sins that have been affecting our families, coworkers, and neighbors. It is well known that if we fast from a certain food for a time, its pull over our will is lessened. We can come to simply pass up those certain foods and not experience the craving as intensely as before the discipline of fasting began. In other words, we *lose the taste* for a certain food after we fast from it for a while. We can actually gain control over the quantity and type of food we enjoy.

In a similar manner, choosing the season of Lent as the time to forego a particular sin may be the optimum time to cooperate with grace and realize this sin's receding power over us. During Lent, the Sunday Scripture readings are filled with encouragement about conversion. Weekday Masses can deepen our resolve, as we come to know daily the transformational power of the Eucharist. Many parishes sponsor adult education forums and vesper services during Lent. There is also the increased opportunity to celebrate the sacrament of reconciliation, and to participate in service or volunteer work. The whole Church conspires to assist its members with moral conversion during Lent.

Attendance at lenten worship services is paramount in the quest for moral conversion, because over time it is the liturgy that forms our affections and directs us to love God. Out of this love, our minds think anew, and old patterns of thought and previously ill-suited objects of our love and attention are replaced by authentic love of God. This powerful reorientation of what we love occurs most objectively at the Mass. It is there that our prayers enter the prayer of Jesus upon the cross. This cross is the prayer of his life being offered in love to his Father, and for love of us and our salvation. In other words, in the Eucharist we are at the very source of Love itself—the heart of Christ offered to God the Father.

In choosing to repent of a particular sin during the lenten season, we embark on a journey to repent from other sins as well. We cannot, for long, offer one sin to be healed in the mercy of God without that mercy touching and transforming our other faults. Christ wants us to give our whole person over to him, not simply individual acts.

For some, in the early stages of moral conversion, Christ is seen as a threat: "What more does this God want from me?" God wants a relationship with us, not simply the satisfaction of seeing us perform good deeds. God wants to love us, and to transform us from within so that we may know the true glory of our lives: intimate and everlasting love with God in the communion of saints.

The ultimate meaning of fasting is its connection to self-forgetfulness. In the early stages of fasting, we will be anything *but* self-forgetful. We will pine for the pleasure of food and drink. As time goes by, however, the space that we formerly filled with food can be filled with other realities. Perhaps an estranged sibling will come to mind and we will be called to reconciliation; or maybe we will begin to see that serving the needs of our family is a primary way to grow in holiness, where earlier their needs had been seen as a burden to endure. In the initial suffering of fasting, we may be invited to seek God in prayer and, hence, a space for God will open more widely in our life.

Fasting is a choice to leave a time of day vacant that is usually filled with personal satisfaction. It reminds us that life is bigger than our personal satisfaction, and it begins a process of self-forgetfulness that later can bloom into authentic service to others. It facilitates the virtue of charity. Fasting teaches us that we can forego constantly thinking of the self and not be threatened with a loss of any significant value. Lent is the season that emphasizes that the less we are concerned with the self, the more space we leave for God to act on our behalf and for us to act on the behalf of others.

Meditation Room:

Giving up something that we cling to
is simply practice for dying.
We claim so many things as "ours" so quickly
(even "our" space in the pew at Sunday Mass).
Can we learn to be free from these inordinate claims?

Almsgiving

Acting on behalf of others is most appropriately symbolized in the traditional activity of almsgiving. As we develop a genuine self-love through the denial of selfish desires, we come to see more clearly not simply the goodness of the self, whom God loves so deeply, but also the goodness of others around us. We come to see others in our lives as both dignified and worthy of respect simply because of their existence. These other persons have needs, and the Church has traditionally called us to be mindful of those needs, especially during Lent. In this way, we are called to give alms. The practice of almsgiving is quite ancient, and seems tied to the very origin of religion in its communal dimension.

Scripture regularly calls us to remember and have mercy upon those who lack what is needed to live a decent life (see, for example, Deuteronomy 15:11 and Proverbs 3:27-28). We truly live out our identity as *imago Dei* (Genesis 1:27) when we show care for those in need. In almsgiving, we mirror God's goodness to us. God, in turn, draws close to us. "Give alms from your possessions, and do not let your eye begrudge the gift when you make it. Do not turn your face away from anyone who is poor, and the face of God will not be turned away from you....for almsgiving delivers from death and keeps you from going into the Darkness" (Tobit 4:7,10).

Almsgiving saves us from the meaninglessness of the self-absorbed life. It is a tangible expression of our faith in a God who cares for our welfare, and we extend God's presence to the world as we cooperate with the grace of showing compassion. As 1 John 3:17 asks: "How does God's love abide in anyone who has the world's goods and sees a brother or sister in need and yet refuses help?"

Elsewhere, I have noted how giving alms spontaneously builds up our disposition to be generous without being overly analytical about how our money will be used by the recipients. Will they spend it on food or alcohol, housing or gambling? (*Pure Heart, Clear Conscience: Living a Catholic Moral Life*, IN: Our Sunday Visitor Publishing [1999] 105). To some extent, these questions only serve to make us stingy in moments where spontaneous and limited personal giving symbolizes our presence, albeit a fleeting one, to the beggar on the street.

For larger donations to individuals or groups, it is only prudent to discern how much we can give in light of legitimate needs. We ought not give unto our own deprivation, except in extraordinary situations. For example, many founders of religious orders began their new life in Christ by giving *all* away to the poor, thereby becoming poor themselves as a witness to God's providential concern. These founders' lives become a bold image of how thinking of others allows God, through the mercy of others, to think of our needs as well. *That* we are to give to people in need is a deep obligation out of Christian charity; *how much* we give has always been a prudent decision based upon our life's circumstances.

Virtue, of course, calls us to be honest about our circumstances and not use this principle to circumvent the necessity of giving. Scripture is clear that holding on to wealth beyond our needs is clinging to useless things. Wealth is meant to be at the service of the poor (James 5:1ff.). This service can take various paths, directly giving to those in need or utilizing wealth to create opportunities for the poor (such as employment, scholarships, grants, even investments for those who have their basic needs unmet). Being creative with existing wealth and being virtuous in the ways of creating new wealth can both be ways to serve the poor. To the extent that virtue allows and is possible, the poor should, themselves, be brought into any decision-making process about their real needs; these cannot be assumed by the giver.

The practice of almsgiving is not a seasonal tradition that ends with Easter Sunday, of course, any more than prayer and fasting are confined only to the lenten season. Almsgiving initiates an entirely new disposition toward our wealth and the presence of the poor among us, which becomes part of our character throughout life. To share wealth with the poor is not the condescending act of one who is superior, but the merciful response to a brother or sister in need from one who knows his or her own dependency upon God. Both rich and poor, in light of the revelation of Christ, know that they share a communion in merciful love. This communion is known and celebrated and made deeper in common worship.

Meditation Room

In his Letter to Hedibian, Saint Jerome wrote that alms should be given as if the giver were the real recipient. What do you think he meant by that?

Communal Worship

As lay people, it is important to try to cultivate a religious imagination about daily life. Monks and nuns have immersed themselves in a domestic culture that is saturated with symbols of God's near and abiding presence. Even the monastery itself, with its physical symbols of chapels, statues, icons, and other religious imagery, helps them remember the holiness of life. Can we remember the holiness of our lives each day? Are there signs, symbols, and rituals from which we can draw life, so that what is good about our secular lives does not get overwhelmed by the perversions of secularism? Can we avoid developing an attitude that denies there is transcendent meaning in the nooks and crannies of ordinary days?

Communal worship speaks to this need. We usually imagine worship as a break in our secular lives, or sometimes even an obstacle to achieving other goals. With this attitude, worship is sometimes simply seen as "time out" from what is really important. Without denying the importance of secular realities for the laity, could we look at worship in another way? Worship is not an obstacle to daily living; it is not time off from more vital realities. Worship is, in fact, the great doorway into all that is both secular and holy. It is our way into real living. In worship, we find the great integration of the simple, ordinary, and plain (people, bread, wine, words) with the holy and transcendent (paschal mystery, incarnation, grace, transformation, salvation). The call of the laity is to carry into each day of work and domestic commitment the truth that *the ordinary and the holy are not opposed*. Only sin and the holy are opposed. Lenten worship services help us bring this truth to the world.

The more we come to see the presence of Christ in worship as a presence that permeates our being in the world, the more we will hunger to participate in worship as the source of our moral witness in everyday life. The Eucharist primarily is our participation in Christ's Paschal Mystery, which is his self-offering to the Father, both in his life and upon the cross, and is also the Father's response in raising him from the dead. Christ came to us; he came to dwell upon Earth and take on created goodness so that all in creation that is not good (sin) may be transformed by his presence, by grace. We too, in communion with him through the grace of the sacramental life, fill the ordinary world with his presence and become witnesses to this salvation through virtue and grace cooperating in moral activity.

A key Scripture reading during the lenten season is the transfiguration story. In this story, Jesus was revealed to the disciples as the favored son of the Father as he was "transfigured before them, and his face shone like the sun, and his clothes became dazzling white" (Matthew 17:2). During this manifestation of the divinity of Christ, God the Father was heard to say: "This is my Son, the Beloved; with him I am well pleased; listen to him!" (Matthew 17:5). If we wish the pleasure or grace of God to rest upon us, we need to listen to the Father. This listening is accomplished primarily in the eucharistic liturgy, and in the *liturgy of our lives* as offered to God.

The Christian life consists mainly in cooperating with grace by going through Christ to the Father. The doorway to that union with the Father is through the listening and responding we do to God's Word, Christ. This Word is proclaimed each Sunday at Mass, and our hearts are to be as attentive to its truth as the disciples were to the transfigured Christ upon the mountain. The entire mystery of Christ comes to be seen through the reality of two mountains, this mount of transfiguration and the mount of Calvary. On the mount of transfiguration, Christ's divinity is revealed, and on Calvary his humanity becomes inescapable, thus leaving the fullness of his identity as the *God/man* to be heralded in the final act of revelation by the Father: the Resurrection.

Our worship at Mass represents this entire mystery of Christ in time, so that we may have access to its truths and love the One who brings us into communion with the Father. It is in this act of worship that sinners find the needed grace to prevail over mortal sin and forgiveness for venial sins. In communal worship, we find not an interrupting of our lives but an entryway into the heart of living as being one with God and one another, a shaded but real prefigurement of eternal life.

Prayer, fasting, almsgiving, and worship constitute the core means of lenten moral conversion. Through these practices, we are brought to yield over inordinate self-love and trust in God, to take up a more healthy love of self in the sight of God's mercy.

Meditation Room:

Communal worship prefigures our place
together in heaven around God.
Can we pray to hasten the reign of God upon Earth,
so that the transition between the here and the hereafter
will not be so jarring?

Conclusion

The season of Lent is a great blessing upon the Church. This season, which begins with the solemn yet simple ceremonies and fasting of Ash Wednesday, culminates in our heart's desire: the hoped-for promise of eternal life with God through the Resurrection of Jesus Christ. There is no more potent drama on Earth than the one participated in through the liturgies and disciplines of Lent. During this time, we may commit ourselves to many personal goals, but the Church especially points to one—the moral conversion of believers. During the Ash Wednesday service, the priest says this: "Father in heaven, the light of your truth bestows sight to the darkness of sinful eyes. May this season of repentance bring us the blessing of your forgiveness and the gift of your light" (Opening Prayer, Ash Wednesday Mass, in *The Sacramentary*, NY: Catholic Book Publishing [1985] 76).

The goal of the Church's call to moral conversion is the joy of living in virtue, a virtue both worked for and received in the mysterious relationship we have with God in Christ. Therefore, the goal of moral conversion truly is our heart's desire, the desire to live our true identity as loved and forgiven children of God. The season of Lent is full of the graces needed to see that such a tragic failure as mortal sin will never be known by any of us, so let us enter into this season deeply, with hearts wide open.

In the end, Lent is something we go through together, as the elderly man in the barber shop—whom I wrote of as we began this journey together—both longed for and remembered from his own youth. We go through the desert together in Christ, and together we can overcome sin in Christ as well. We learn that only together can our real spiritual and material needs be met, and that our conversions are facilitated by our communal life. Let's not just leave Lent to Ash Wednesday and Holy Week, but rather live it fully each day, and cooperate with the graces of communal living at home, in the parish, and in civil society.

This desert of Lent will come to an end. It will open up to the fresh water of Easter time, when all things of God come to life and are sustained by divine goodness. We are called to drink deeply of this life-giving water.